Syllabus

Syllabus

The Remarkable, Unremarkable Document That Changes Everything

William Germano
& Kit Nicholls

Princeton University Press

Princeton and Oxford

Requests for permission to reproduce material from this work
should be sent to permissions@press.princeton.edu

Published by Princeton University Press
41 William Street, Princeton, New Jersey 08540
6 Oxford Street, Woodstock, Oxfordshire OX20 1TR

press.princeton.edu

Library of Congress Cataloging-in-Publication Data

Names: Germano, William P., [date] author. | Nicholls, Kit, [date] author.
Title: Syllabus : the remarkable, unremarkable document that changes
    everything / William Germano and Kit Nicholls.
Description: Princeton : Princeton University Press, [2020] |
    Includes bibliographical references and index.
Identifiers: LCCN 2020017920 | ISBN 9780691192208 (hardback) |
    ISBN 9780691209876 (ebook)
Subjects: LCSH: Education, Higher—Curricula. | Curriculum planning. |
    College teaching.
Classification: LCC LB2361 .G45 2020 | DDC 378.1/99—dc23
LC record available at https://lccn.loc.gov/2020017920

British Library Cataloging-in-Publication Data is available

Editorial: Peter Dougherty and Alena Chekanov
Production Editorial: Sara Lerner
Text Design: Leslie Flis
Jacket Design: Jessica Massabrook
Production: Erin Suydam
Publicity: Amy Stewart and James Schneider
Copyeditor: Amy K. Hughes

This book has been composed in Minion Pro

Printed on acid-free paper. ∞

Printed in the United States of America

10 9 8 7 6 5 4 3 2 1

to students

Plans are useless, but planning is everything.
—Attributed to Dwight David Eisenhower, who
attributed it to an old soldier. No idea where the
old soldier got it. So much for sources.

Contents

Acknowledgments

Books happen to writers because of the people around them. That's not the whole story, of course, but it's a lot of the story. There are some people without whom this book would be impossible to imagine, at least in the way you're seeing it. Peter Dougherty, former director at Princeton University Press and now editor at large, exercised his abundant and persuasive good cheer, and Christie Henry, director of the press, gave this book an essential thumbs up. Tanya McKinnon of McKinnon Literary guided this boat to safe harbor. We want to thank the anonymous readers for Princeton, whose enthusiasm for the project was leavened with just the right quantity of suggestions for pointing and underlining what we had tried to say.

Each of us has a circle of colleagues and friends with whom we've had seemingly endless conversations about teaching. Those circles overlap, but their independence from one another gives this project multiple points of origin. Some of those colleagues have worked specifically on questions of education. Others just do the work in the classroom as thoughtfully as they can. Some do both.

As a start, John Lundberg, Pam Newton, and all of our colleagues in the Center for Writing at the Cooper Union have given us a teaching home these past few years. Pat C. Hoy and Gwen Hyman taught one of these authors most of what he knows about teaching, and Mary Poovey, John Waters, Leeore Schnairson, Beth Machlan, Amy Hosig, and too many mentors and colleagues to name here probably taught him the rest.

During his time working as a publisher, the other author tried to figure out how books can say something and even teach something. (Books are funny that way: They teach you things if you let them.) With authors and colleagues and friends—the lines can blur in good ways—a lifetime of conversations about ideas forms the background of this book. Everyone at the Center for Writing continues to teach this teacher, demonstrating the same principle of critical generosity we write about in the pages that follow. For assistance, advice, and conversations they may not remember (but this coauthor does), thanks go to Nick Tampio, bell hooks, Greg Britton, AnaLouise Keating, and Carla O. Alvarez and the Gloria Anzaldúa Archive.

And then there's still more to learn, because, as we'll suggest in a dozen different ways, teaching is a kind of knowledge— like all kinds of knowledge—that never sits still. We've learned a lot of the "still more" from our families. T. Charnan Lewis has been teaching Kit with varying degrees of success for fifteen years and counting, and Zora Nicholls taught Kit that, as we'll say later (with no less ambiguity), the art of teaching is hope, as an art. Dan and Dawn Nicholls sit at the origin point of everything Kit has done and have offered continued wisdom and grace throughout his life.

Bill, as the other author is frequently called, wonders how the people living with the person who is doing the writing manage to put up with it, since writing is, after all, a thief of time. Diane Gibbons has given—taught—William (she's never liked the name Bill) too much to name here and done so with incomprehensible patience and so much more, over many years. Our son Chris is now out in the world with a life of his own, but he will remember well how these writing projects take over one's home. What part of a life isn't teaching and learning if you want it to be? Let wordless gratitude, as well as wordful love, be noted here.

As teachers, we owe most to our students, and that means not only the best and brightest we've had the privilege to teach but also the ones for whom the class was—on many levels—a challenge. Testing one's teaching chops against what the most successful student accomplishes is too easy. Figuring out why something doesn't work, or why a student is struggling, is surely a better route for understanding what's at stake in education. That's a polite way of saying that moments of unsuccessful teaching are crucial to learning *as a teacher.* So if it were possible, we'd like to thank all our students in some sort of large-scale chronological order, from those we met in our first fumbling moments as TAs to the students we're just getting to know at the start of another term. From them we have learned much about what education means and how it works. But just as important, our students have taught us much about what education *isn't* and what *doesn't* work. The focus of this book—its subject, center, and hope—is our students and yours.

Preface: Reality Check

When one of us was in graduate school, two young assistant professors of English were writing an ambitious and very long book together. That was *The Madwoman in the Attic*, a now-classic work of feminist literary criticism (the title is an allusion to Charlotte Brontë's *Jane Eyre*, in which a still-living wife is the male protagonist's inconvenient secret).[1] The authors, Susan Gubar and Sandra Gilbert, quickly became major figures in their field, and their book and ideas endure. What was especially impressive—astonishing, really—was that although they drafted portions of the book separately, their conversations about and through those drafts resulted in a text that was *theirs*. Their book is a collaboration and a conversation, or rather, the resulting trace of collaborations and conversations. The hand of either might be in any part of it.

Decades later, the book you're reading now was written by two people, working together in such a way that, going back through their text, they are not always sure who has written what. This much is clear: One of us proposed the book as an idea and inveigled the other into the scheme. That may sound like nothing much, but it's uncommon in the humanities and social sciences. Scientific fields regularly produce academic papers with multiple authors. Sometimes a scholarly report no more than a few data-heavy pages in length is crowned by a parade of authors, in which the position of one's name beneath the title signals something about the importance of one's contribution. Humanists don't tend to write this way.

---

[1] Sandra Gilbert and Susan Gubar, *The Madwoman in the Attic: The Woman Writer and the Nineteenth-Century Literary Imagination* (New Haven, CT: Yale University Press, 1979).

One of the mantras of modern-day teaching is the institutional value placed on collaborative pedagogy. *Collaborative teaching*—these days a bit of a magic word literally indicating some form of working together—is meant to indicate not merely two or more people teaching together but two or more people *teaching together to accomplish something not yet present in the curriculum and not remotely possible if done by either one working alone.* Collaboration in this sense, then, is different from task-sharing. "You wash, I'll dry" is good kitchen collaboration but not at all what we mean here. To put that in writerly terms, collaboration isn't deciding who writes which chapters. In teacherly terms, it isn't deciding who teaches which weeks of a semester in a course billed as demonstrating collaborative pedagogy. That's not what we did, and not what we want to explore.

In thinking together about this project, we each had a hunch that the other had something more and different to contribute, that the other had an access, a way of thinking about the problem, that might yield something useful on the page. We quickly realized that the work of writing would have to be collaborative in the Gubar and Gilbert sense of interwoven prose. Somehow, we wrote together, often working live on laptops across a dining room table in an old, chilly house, with lots of coffee and music quietly playing. Sometimes we wrote at work, stealing a space where our other obligations might not find us for an hour, in which we could hammer out what we thought about how to rethink a classroom's patterns and habits. We engaged in frenetic exchanges of text messages, caffeinated walks near campus, stochastic bouts of rewriting the same paragraph ad nauseam until the words somehow landed in patterns we didn't hate. And always we circled the same thing: what it's really like to teach at a college, and how to try to do it well.

As our bios say, we both work at The Cooper Union for the Advancement of Science and Art, a small private college in New York City. There are no liberal arts majors, so our teaching isn't about winning majors for a department. Maybe a poor environment for academics intent on training the next generation of humanist academics, but it's also an environment that you can use to test pedagogy and to figure out, class by class and student by student, what counts and why. We're colleagues. As you already know, the mere fact of working at the same institution in itself guarantees little if the goal is to make collegiality a real thing rather than an empty sentiment. But we came to see that we each wanted to work more on questions of teaching, the classroom, and what the idea of the university was all about—a big and familiar topic, as any issue of the *Chronicle of Higher Education* makes clear.

Collaboration is deliberately messy, intentionally prone to a certain kind of disorder out of which a perhaps unanticipated result may emerge. In a sense, collaboration has something in common with the determined chaos of revising a text—it's a process of thinking and rethinking, and taking risks while doing it. From a different angle, collaboration has something in common with the task of helping students understand how writing works and how their own thinking generates their own writing. Not coincidentally, we both teach. Also not coincidentally, one of us writes about publishing and revising writing, and one of us directs a writing center. That we trusted one another implicitly is hardly a given (we're academics, after all), but we did, even trusting one another to think about what could be done better, even going so far as to throw out whole paragraphs, pages, or even fully drafted chapters. We each taught the other.

A lot of smart people have tried to write about teaching. Some, like John Dewey and, later, Paolo Freire, have guided the way in which the classroom must be rethought. Others, like bell hooks and a generation of alert, often activist critical thinkers, have urged us all to rethink more, more often, differently. This book is a small contribution in a big field—Princeton, Chicago, Harvard, Johns Hopkins, Yale, NYU, West Virginia, Teachers College—these are only some of the academic houses that have made questions of teaching questions for everyone. That it's a big field is a sign that people recognize the need. Smaller commercial presses as well as big trade houses are also part of the conversation, as they should be. Thinking about teaching is thinking about learning, which means it's a subject that touches all our lives.

What does this book aim to do? A few things. Teaching students anything involves a particular value—let's call it critical generosity—that sits balanced on the knife edge between judgment and endorsement. You want students to argue and evaluate arguments, and you want them to do that while acknowledging something deeply humane in anything we humans try to make, or do, or say. When it works, collaboration engages, among other things, this critical generosity. That is, there are values that undergird something as simple as reading someone else's poem or as complicated as writing a book with a colleague. Or maybe as simple as collaborating on a book and as complex as reading a poem.

The book that lies ahead is about collaboration, though we didn't begin by articulating that to ourselves as we were writing it. (Of course, this book collaborates with the thinking that has gone before it.) The collaboration that *Syllabus* examines is shared work in a quite specific sense: work *between* and *among* students within the dispensation of the classroom, and work between students and teacher. We'll put it more strongly, too: *Syllabus* is, in fact, not about the possibility of such a collaboration but the *necessity* of it. It's a book about designing conditions and structures, dynamics and experiments, in which students can learn. The teacher may seem to be doing less—most of the hard work is invisible, the way ordinary classroom prep is invisible. The difference in the pedagogical design we're proposing is that as teachers we name and act on the necessity of engaging our students not only in "our" subject but in "their" work.

The syllabus is just the starting point. Dynamics are adjusted. Students do more, think more. Clocks still count, but classroom time is apportioned in different ways. A teacher's authority isn't diminished, but the work of teaching feels different, and in academia different is often a source of professional anxiety.

"So you want to change what I've been doing in the classroom—quite successfully, I believe—for three (or thirty) years?" Wildly risky, you're probably thinking, and we don't disagree with you. What could it mean to collaborate with those you're engaged to teach? Scientists frequently collaborate with their most advanced students; directors of laboratories plan on sharing responsibility for a research project. Teachers in massive courses often have teaching assistants, emerging scholars who might be thought of as the teachers' collaborators. But to collaborate with students? What would that mean? Over the past twenty years there's been a lot of work on what the classroom should be and how it should work. Large classrooms and small, digital and physical, and for each there have been good suggestions and not so good ones. We won't rehearse it all here—that would be a history of thinking about teaching today. The best moments in that history, though, would put special value on collaboration, and that's where we want to connect to the larger conversation about teaching.

We're proposing a way of thinking about teaching that is meant to function both as a paradigm and as a practical guide, something any teacher can try on and try out. Over the course of the book we've placed some suggestions for prompts for your students, and some prompts for you, the teacher, too. Use them if they work. Adjust them as you need to. They're tools. Our objective is to take the syllabus—that almost invisible bureaucratic document—and use it to think about students' learning, students' lives, the urgency many of us feel that classrooms have to work better than they do.

The classroom has already been, has always been, a space of collaboration, even if those collaborations have often been unsuccessful or unrecognized. We wanted to help ourselves and our readers think about how to guide collaborations toward success.

We came to an awareness that the difference between teaching and learning is, like so many binary oppositions, often an illusion. Each of us has experienced the event of teaching as a learning event (cue Chaucer's clerk, and gladly would he teach and gladly learn), and every good teacher goes into the arena of teaching—the classroom, the studio, the seminar, the lecture hall, the laboratory, the rehearsal room—not just to give but to take away, too. Or rather, there's much to be gained by seeing the border between teaching and learning as a messy, badly policed, even playful trading zone in which the person called the teacher invents ways to pull the students and the subject into a deeper, more complex relationship, one in which it's the students themselves who can, despite the limits of their subject knowledge, reshape what teachers understand of the subject. As this book argues, understanding a subject is perhaps even more about *how* than about *what*. Helping students engage questions and histories, methods and theories and possibilities makes us do the same in new ways. Good teachers know how much their students teach them. We're just building here on that awareness.

A book built from a real collaboration feels as if it should itself be some sort of model, a way of working from which patterns of messy productivity might be deduced. We're not sure, though, that anything so comfortingly straightforward is possible. Maybe it's enough to declare that this collaboratively written book takes as its aim the classroom's essential dynamic and the document that lays out the rules for that dynamic. And that the negotiations involved in our writing process produced a book that—like a successful syllabus— imagines its readers as collaborators, too.

To rethink the syllabus sounds like a small thing—and it is, if your only objective is a clearer, more efficient syllabus. But as will be obvious by now, that's not what this book is about. We wanted to write about the most urgent thing of all: what happens in the classroom. The syllabus just happens to be the classroom's point of entry, timekeeper, and compass. Everything else about your teaching—from anxiety dreams to writing assignments, from understanding testing and what it's for to your choice of readings and what students are going to do with them—are folded into the innocuous document we hand out at the first class meeting.

Teaching is always collaborative, maybe especially so when there's only one teacher at the front of the room. If you're that teacher, your collaborators are in front of you, in rows or a circle, squeezed around a seminar table or arranged in stadium seating, or maybe online and only visible in digital form. If you teach, this is a book meant to tell truths about what we do, in a way that you can recognize and use. But, of course, students make a class possible, so *Syllabus* is—not finally, but from the start—about and for them.

About and *for*, subject and object. Real collaborative learning, collaborative teaching, collaborative writing, messing up comfortable borders. There's no formula, only strategies and sometimes shareable insights.

How should you use *Syllabus*? As we tell our students, write in your book. Just be sure it's yours first. And take your time.

In fact, we hope you'll read it all, but slowly. A chapter a day or every couple of days as you rethink a syllabus seems both far more productive and far more humane than inhaling it in one sitting.

One of our goals is to make you want to think about how you think about teaching. A few centuries ago, you might have opened a book and found at the top of a section something labeled "the Argument"—a summary, if you like, and a pointer to what readers might want to keep their eyes on.[2] At the start of each of our chapters, you'll find our versions of the pointed summary: a question or questions addressed to you, the teacher. We hope you'll think of them less as assignments and more as prompts for your own thinking or—better—for your own writing.

In some important sense, then, this is a book that remains necessarily incomplete. It can only ever offer a framework, an armature, on which your experiences, your difficulties, your theories will build. We hope that diligent readers, thinking about these prompts throughout the book, will compose their own version of *Syllabus*, one that will turn the tables, so to speak, and make students of teachers and teachers of students.

As we finish copyediting, we and teachers everywhere are living through a historic disruption in our teaching practices due to COVID-19, yet another reminder that everything about teaching is always contingent, always subject to (sometimes radical) change. This book's focus remains squarely on your own thinking about your students—not on us "delivering" a single program for teaching. Online or in person, in crisis or

---

[2] In the seventeenth century, Milton's publisher coaxed him to provide "Arguments" for the books into which *Paradise Lost* is divided. For more than three centuries, Milton's readers have been grateful. In the world of modern anthologies, an editor selects materials for inclusion and often prefaces each selection with a headnote. Anthology readers, especially students, have been grateful for these, too.

in the mundane grind of another term, teaching is about process, not object.

Writing this book therefore became a learning laboratory of two, without formulas, built around an idea of collaboration, which has a lot to do with our ideas about teaching and learning. It became not only a joint project but a gift each was able to give the other. (Two teachers, two students.) We hope it's a gift to you and to your students as well.

Syllabus

1

What You Do, What They Do

What really *is* a syllabus? Is it a tool or a manifesto?
A machine or a plan? What are its limits? Its horizon?
And who is it really for? And what would happen if
you took the syllabus as seriously as you take the most
serious forms of writing in your own discipline?

It's so familiar. The first day, the first class meeting, the noises,
the competing interests of choosing seats and choosing neighbors, the geometry of students and backpacks, tools, food,
books. For you, it's curtain up. You've brought with you a set
of handouts, the ones you quickly say are also and always
available online in the course learning module. You distribute the handouts, making eye contact as you do it—everyone
is so young, and the class is more diverse each time you steal
a glance. You're looking for their response, even before they've
read a word of what you've set down.

You remind yourself that your students are there for one
of two reasons. Either they have to be there, or they want to
be there. Either your course is a) required of everyone or
maybe required in some specific track, or b) it's an elective.
You know that neither category guarantees an easy ride, and
you wouldn't want it any other way. Teaching is hard. One of
your goals is to have the students who have to be there want
to be there. Another goal is surely to make students who
choose your course tell others that it was amazing, that you

were terrific. Teaching is hard, you tell yourself again. Knowing that is part of being a teacher.

You feel the electricity of performance, the responsibility of winning students over to your discipline. You run through what you're going to say this hour in a distracted, internal monologue. A few moments later, and the class has settled down into what looks like an attentive reading of the handout. It feels as if it's your moment to lose: students poring over the little world you've created for them, a place where the hierarchy of the university—your mastery, their innocent but open-minded ignorance—is mediated by a simple document and the set of rules to which it conforms. Their eyes turn to you. Electronics are stowed. You pick up a piece of chalk. House lights down. You begin. You will be at that blackboard, chalk in hand, for sixteen weeks, and during that time your voice, and your brilliance, will fill the space.

You begin talking, but something strange is happening. All your expertise seems to have left you, and you're jabbering on in what you recognize as a steady stream of amateurish nonsense. But that's not the most horrifying part. What's truly frightening is that the students are looking at you as if you're making perfect sense—or, more accurately, as if it doesn't matter whether you're brilliant or banal.

Then the alarm clock goes off and you wake up. It's four a.m., still dark, and you don't have to be on campus for another two weeks. You spent last night fine-tuning your syllabus one last time and in the process ratcheting up your own anxiety.

You've just awakened from one version of the Academic's Performance Dream. In the dream-class, you were about to *tell the students something* for sixteen weeks, which might be fine if your course were a one-way transmission to an adoring audience and nothing more. You wouldn't really teach a class that way.

And yet you're beginning to concede that the dream that woke you is more or less a critique—*your* critique—of your own teaching, your unconscious mind accusing you of a particular kind of earnest, hardworking—what to call it?—laziness. You're half-awake now and recognize too much of your own teaching style. It isn't a horror show—far from it. Reasonably genial, largely inert, a series of solos in which you enacted knowledge of the subject, underscoring memorable points with chalk, points dutifully copied by a silent room of students whose own thoughts remained locked away for the semester or at least until the final exam.

The sun's coming up, and your morning resolution is not to teach that way again. You're not even sure what kind of teaching that was, but it felt deeply incomplete. You're awake now and, breaking the rules you've set for yourself, you've got your laptop open in bed. You're anxiously looking over that syllabus one more time. Is it too much, too little, too complicated, too filled with arrows that point the student to side roads? Could you read your own syllabus and make a reasonable guess as to what the course wants to accomplish, as opposed to what your department's course catalogue says that the course studies or describes? Could you recognize what the course challenges students to do? And how exactly would you, the teacher who wrote that syllabus, follow through on your own expectations for students?

Dreaming or waking, these questions never seem to go away. Teachers aim high. Big targets, big goals. A class that sings with intellectual engagement. Rigorous but fair grading, and each student doing better than you had hoped. The gratification of giving the exemplary lecture to a room of attentive students. Your own delight in the difficulty that comes with thinking seriously about things that count. All good goals, which, taken together, add up to an ideal of the teacher-focused class. "You're a star!" says somebody in the hallway, possibly without irony.

But stars are bright, distant things, and the light they throw off is old, old news. What might it mean to teach now, to shine now, in the present, close to the moment and our students? This question is about more than diversity or age or ethnic sensitivity or a sympathetic engagement with the complexities of gender, or disability, or any of the other qualities that distinguish person from person. First or last, teaching is inevitably about all of these things.[1] But to be present asks that we do so much more. Our students, hungry for something that starry light can't provide by itself, need from us not just knowledge—even knowledge tempered by sensitivity—but craft.

The myth of Prometheus—the Greek name means "forethought"—tells us that this most generous of Titans stole fire from the gods and brought it to us clay-built human creatures, functionally kindling life in our dark world. Teaching in the present is a bit like stealing fire. Here, o starry teacher, the fire is your own but briefly. Teaching is renouncing the glamour and assurance of the well-executed solo and sharing that light with your students, moving the focus from something we've long called teaching and giving the torch to learning. You can teach by yourself, or at least tell yourself that you can, but you can't *learn* (let's for a moment allow it to be a transitive verb meaning "to make them learn") by yourself.

Modern English *learn* has as one of its antecedents the Old English form *gelaeran*, which meant "to teach." This etymological paradox isn't a paradox at all, of course. If teaching is the thing that happens when students are learning, subject and object come to be bound together, like Aristophanes's

---

[1] The randomness of a class's enrollment is a teacher's first, and recurring, lesson in life, and it's a good thing, too.

conception of the sexes balled up inseparably in *The Symposium*, a Möbius-like continuum of teaching and learning, enacted by teacher and student.

We begin to discern the contours of this perplexing space of learning when we awake from the dream (it was always only a dream, never a solid reality) of the masterful teacher delivering knowledge. We can map out something so complex only by making a concerted effort to describe its nuances, conundrums, its areas of density and lightness. We perform this mapping and engage in this forethought when we compose a syllabus, but only if it is indeed an attempt to map the space of learning. Which means that, as we'll say in several ways throughout this book, a syllabus isn't so much about what you will do. It's about what your students will do.

The Syllabus We Have

The syllabus is the most remarkable, unremarkable document in the history of education. We depend on it as if it were always there, always reliable, always true. We depend on it as a transparent summary of what a classroom can and must accomplish. Some few are better than others. Most aren't nearly as good as the best. The syllabus as we traditionally know it may read as if it's all about what *will* happen in the next sixteen weeks, but to a great extent it's really about what the teacher has experienced as recently as last year and as long ago as graduate school. A teacher crafts a syllabus based on the teacher's own prior experience as a student, in conversation with peers, as a result of the bruises and exaltations last time teaching the course, or some combination of all three.

The traditional syllabus is that starry, bright light from the past shining into today's classroom, even if it looks as if it's news. (Prospero's response to Miranda in *The Tempest*—"Tis new to thee"—is a phrase you may have heard to describe a student's response to something, but Prospero's not the most reflective character in Shakespeare.) It's never enough, then, for a syllabus to be, as one often hears, "freshened up" for another semester.

The word *syllabus* itself has a curious history. The *Oxford English Dictionary* helps us see *syllabus* as not just a word but a scribal mistake. The story of *syllabus* stretches back to the fourteenth century, when Petrarch was gathering everything he could find of Cicero's writings. Among the period's discoveries were the so-called Medicean manuscripts, which contained Cicero's letters, including those to his great friend Titus Pomponius Atticus. In one of the letters to Atticus (the document in question is Cicero Epp. ad Atticum iv. iv.), the word *sillabos* appears. As the *OED* explains, in the fifteenth century, editions of Cicero's letters printed the word *syllabus*, "a corrupt reading" of "sittybas or Greek σιττύβας, accusative plural of sittyba, σιττύβα parchment label or title-slip on a book." From the corrupt reading, scholars posited "a spurious σύλλαβος," which was then treated as a derivative of the verb συλλαμβάνειν, "to put together, collect." Every mention of every syllabus since then can be traced back to the misreading of one classical manuscript. So is it *syllabuses* or *syllabi*? There's probably not much point in worrying about the correct plural of an "ancient" word that was accidentally invented in the fifteenth century.

The Google Books Ngram Viewer, which scans the contents of some five million books, records the first significant appearance of *syllabus* in the second half of the eighteenth century. That would suggest that the concept of the syllabus is one of the Enlightenment's many undertakings. It's not until the period after World War I, however, that *syllabus* begins its meteoric rise. The word itself is almost a synonym for the methodical organization of modern educational practice: Syllabus equals authority, or at least stands as authority's flag.

From the Enlightenment through the middle of the twentieth century, the syllabus was most often understood as a table of contents—or simply the content—of a course, a listing of the expert knowledge that the professor would deliver to students. The syllabus has even been invested with a religious aura; the OED records one definition of the term as "a summary statement of points decided and errors condemned by ecclesiastical authority," a usage with its own surprising history.

In 1864, the papacy of Pius IX issued a "Syllabus errorum"— *syllabus* here meaning simply a list, or catalogue, of condemned practices, attitudes, and opinions. The "Syllabus errorum"—a list of errors, or heresies, that had crept into earlier documents concerning points of theology and other Church matters—culminated in a stance against "progress, liberalism, and modern civilization," clearly meant as a blanket defense against the breaking news of the late nineteenth century.[2] Four decades later, Pope Pius X renewed the Vatican's defenses with another *syllabus*—"Lamentabili sane"—to which the Church gives the explanatory English subtitle "Syllabus Condemning the Errors of the Modernists." "With truly lamentable results," it declares, "our age, casting aside all restraint in its search for the ultimate causes of things, frequently pursues novelties so ardently that it rejects the legacy of the human race."[3]

Neither papal syllabus is meant as a teaching tool in the ordinary sense. They're more like manifestos. In the twenty-first

---

[2] Pope Pius IX, "The Syllabus of Errors," 1864, *Papal Encyclicals Online*, accessed March 23, 2020, https://www.papalencyclicals.net/pius09/p9syll.htm.

[3] Pope Pius X, "*Lamentabili Sane*: Syllabus Condemning the Errors of the Modernists," 1907, *Papal Encyclicals Online*, accessed March 23, 2020, https://www.papalencyclicals.net/Pius10/p10lamen.htm.

century it would be the rare classroom indeed that was organized around a syllabus that included refutation of modernism—much less modernity—as a learning outcome. Though as a teacher you might be tempted to gather up your own catalogue of errors—from common grammatical mistakes to the tried, true, and oh so tired default of the five-paragraph essay—into a classroom handout.[4]

Much of what happens in the classroom involves rules. For those of us who teach, the syllabus is not only document but rule book, canvas, and plan, and perhaps most of all a model for imagining a sphere of operations for a course's ideas. Think for a moment of the armillary spheres that Chinese and then Renaissance astronomers built as they tried to envision the universe. Like this or any model, your syllabus is reductive: It can't possibly name every potential condition, every possible state, that your class will exhibit. (And it may—or maybe even necessarily will—get some things wrong.) But it tries. A social scientist might describe the syllabus as a rule-bound system that attempts to anticipate and induce a set of behaviors in and beyond your classroom. We all have to anticipate and induce.

Now imagine a whole sequence of your syllabi—revisions of the same course from year to year, perhaps over a couple of decades—but animated like a time-lapse film documenting its evolution. Have the syllabi with which you work become more or less accurate—more or less true to the life of real classroom teaching and learning? Many faculty would likely say more, many would say less, and still more would probably find the question odd. Those who say it's become more accurate might argue that the syllabus's growing inclusion of statements

---

[4]John Warner gets to the heart of it in *Why They Can't Write: Killing the Five-Paragraph Essay and Other Necessities* (Baltimore: Johns Hopkins University Press, 2018).

on accommodating student learning differences, counseling resources, and the like better address the needs of our students. Countering such claims, others might argue that administrative impositions on our syllabi are transforming them from something that models how we want our classrooms to operate into something that models the way lawyers or corporate boards see higher education. Many will find the exercise absurd: Syllabi just aren't that important, and other than spelling out requirements, they don't have that much to do with the week-to-week work of a semester.

You've no doubt looked at those quasi-legal (or straightforwardly legal) disclaimers and sections in your syllabi and wondered what they signify about changes in how college education works. Today these are—more explicitly than ever—the rules of classroom behavior, and they are substantial. Here are the HR policies at this institution, the small type containing the recourse a student may have if rules of behavior are violated. Here are the emails and phone numbers that will connect students with necessary resources on and off campus to help with stress, or illness, financial dilemmas, even homelessness. Obligatory paragraphs might cover the precise number of absences permitted, even though every person who teaches (and who therefore commits to showing up to each class meeting) has to suppress disappointment when even a strong student seems to take advantage of the attendance "lenience" that, according to departmental policy, the syllabus must spell out.

Some people talk of forgiveness, as if missing class is a venial sin or civil misdemeanor, while students are more likely to talk of skipping class and taking "excused" absences. Some institutions require that the syllabus contain the entirety of the institution's academic integrity policy, detailing what is and is not plagiarism and the consequences of violating that policy. Sometimes those consequences are spelled out in *first strike, second strike, third strike* terms. Policies, resources and warnings, caveats and urgings.

We recognize that much of this material has emerged in relation to complex problems of power, access, and fairness. Some of the required statements and counseling resources are valuable, if not all of equivalent value, taken one by one. But their presence on the syllabus inevitably moves the document from a plan for learning into a contract for satisfying a degree requirement. The teacher's contribution to the syllabus can seem as if it's crowded out by administrative fine print, so that it's easy to look at a syllabus and think that the three Rs are readings, regulations, and recourse. We're not teachers if we're salespeople servicing customers. The syllabus isn't the warranty on a Toyota. We're not lay therapists or auxiliary police, either. We're teachers.[5]

And yet. What was simple fifty years ago is now complex, deliberate, attentive, and crowded with intentions. The syllabus has become not just a document but a contested space, a space where we can see one of the central forms for planning and carrying out higher learning slipping away from faculty control and, for that matter, from its ideal point of origin: A good syllabus is borne of a real teacher's experiences working with real students. Like any piece of writing, it will be only as good as its ability to communicate urgently and effectively with readers.

---

[5] Change a word and you do, usually, change how you imagine what that word describes. Throughout this book, we'll refer to you, the people doing the teaching, as teachers rather than as professors. This is partly a move that recognizes the many titles contingent faculty bear in the contemporary university—and the friction they feel when a student addresses them as "professor." But it's also an attempt to embrace what is often a marginalized part of our jobs as faculty. You already know the complex reasons for that marginalization. For our purposes, what's important is that, at least in the confines of this book, we grow comfortable imagining ourselves through the language of teaching.

The Syllabus We Could Have

"So why would anyone want to read a book about the syllabus?" We've encountered that question many times in putting this project together. Not necessarily in so many words, of course, but we knew what was implied. And the next question—unspoken or not—becomes, "Why would anyone *write* a book about the syllabus?"

If you look at much of what's been written on the subject of education, it's clear that not many scholars thought that the syllabus itself was worth their readers' time, or their own. Books and articles about teaching, and about the syllabus especially, are often reductive, often clinically abstracted from the realities of our specific disciplinary work. On the one hand, they offer programs for reducing the labor of the classroom to a repertoire of standard actions and protocols. On the other hand, they seem to be part of a conversation among education scholars rather than being written to meet the concerns and needs of teachers themselves. With the best of intentions, such books participate in the work of defining teaching and learning by restricting both, not out of ill will but out of what reads like an unwillingness to acknowledge the lives of real students, in real bodies, engaging real problems, and real texts, taught by real teachers. We often ignore this kind of writing because it feels so very distant from what it's actually like to be in a college—or any—classroom.

Books about teaching are often talking to one another.[6] They are, if you will, books about books about teaching rather than books about the thing we do in the classroom. While so-called learning-centered models of teaching are rooted in

---

[6]The same can, of course, be said about most studies within any scholarly discipline.

important insights coming from dedicated scholars and theorists, these same models have increasingly come to be attached to an administrative discourse that makes many of us uncomfortable. Too much writing about teaching bears more in common with internet listicles ("8 Common Mistakes to Avoid Making in the Classroom," "5 Simple Ways to Increase Student Engagement") than a centuries-old practice we carry forward with a sense of deep responsibility. This piecemeal approach to talking about teaching implies that one can simply drop teaching techniques into an existing course, like installing a plug-in to your internet browser. Teaching isn't like that.

We're trying here to do something that connects directly to both the big picture and the tight close-up of the educational experience. The syllabus seemed to us the nexus of big and tight, the place where philosophical ambitions and epistemological assumptions meet next week's reading assignment and prep for a midterm. The question for us, then, becomes thinking through these multiple goals and constraints. You may be surprised to see, in a book on the syllabus, as much engagement with the everyday of the semester—with lesson plans, with the texture of momentary teaching quandaries, and so on. But like the teaching/learning continuum we described earlier, the distinction between your syllabus and your classroom teaching is far harder to make than a traditional approach to the syllabus permits.

So, we've been asked, "Why not a book on, say, effective teaching, or how to get students to read more in the age of digital distraction?" Our answer is straightforward: There are many kinds of teaching and many environments in which teaching takes place. The syllabus is the constitutive document for these courses of teaching and learning—a thing we make, or should make, any time we hope to bring a body of people into a body of knowledge. And so this book on the syllabus is also a book on effective teaching that begins with your syllabus—*and* a book on getting students to read that starts with the reading list in which your syllabus takes evident pride.

We've spoken with many teachers who find their own college's faculty development efforts in relation to course design lacking—primarily because they feel that these efforts aren't adequate to the specific challenges of teaching what they teach to the real students in their classes. Our sense is that the syllabus needs a reevaluation and, ultimately, a higher status in academic discourse, so that we can use it to answer that question. And this sense has led us to a different way of thinking about it, one that fuses the intellectual ambitions of higher learning with the practical realities of navigating a semester. It's also an approach to the syllabus that tries to honor what we *don't* know (a lot; almost everything) about your discipline, your students, your institution. So how can we imagine a better syllabus, in order to be better teachers?

For starters, let's agree that a syllabus is, above all else, a *design for student work*. Again, it's about what *they* will do, not so much about what you'll do. A steady reform movement has for decades been advocating a different relationship between faculty and students, one in which nurturing and motivating supplants deciding and condemning. The goal becomes to discern what you, the teacher, want your students to be able to do—with a body of knowledge, with a set of disciplinary practices—and to learn or invent ways to get students to do these things. Not only does a great deal of scholarship point to this approach as an effective way to teach, but faculty who have tried it usually find that the everyday experience of teaching is much more intellectually engaging than traditional, more comfortably risk-free, ways of organizing class time.[7]

---

[7]The academic literature on the effectiveness of what is too simply called "active learning" is so robust that it's absurd to attempt to summarize it here. Perhaps it's better to point to works that compile that research: John C. Bean's extremely

To get to intellectual engagement is the big challenge. It's more than great lecturing or dazzling PowerPoint (in fact it's rarely about great lecturing and never about dazzling Power-Point). It's less about polish than you may think, or at least not the kind of polish that we may all have been taught is one hallmark of the Great Teacher. Getting students' attention is part of the job, but circus performers can do that just as well as, if not better than, teachers. We're not advocating red noses and rubber chickens, though if they work for you, that's fine, too.[8] Teaching well is knowing what to do with your students' attention once you have it. It's more than having them shut off their phones and close their laptops. It's breaking up the center of attention so that there are, finally, not one but many centers of attention.

A syllabus is an opportunity to draft a sequence of activities that students will perform in a specific order. Like any time-based medium, the college course needs a narrative, but that narrative will be both enacted and experienced primarily by your students rather than by you. If you're paying attention yourself, every time you teach a course you'll discover new nuances to the story it tells. But those nuances will emerge from the surprising things your students do with the activities—readings, problem sets, labs, essays, performances, presentations, group work, case studies, and more—that you've planned and developed.

---

useful and widely read *Engaging Ideas: The Professor's Guide to Integrating Writing, Critical Thinking, and Active Learning in the Classroom*, 2nd ed. (San Francisco: Jossey-Bass, 2011); Susan A. Ambrose et al., *How Learning Works: Seven Research-Based Principles for Smart Teaching* (San Francisco: Jossey-Bass, 2010); and Peter C. Brown et al., *Make It Stick: The Science of Successful Learning* (Cambridge, MA: Harvard University Press, 2014). The list could go on and on.

[8] A degree of clowning can sometimes help students learn. When we take risks and appear to be the biggest goofball in the room, students often feel more free to take their own risks.

Here's where we want to make a move: What changes if you think of a syllabus as a narrative? A good narrative, as every reader knows, is driven by not-knowing. ("No spoilers!") Every good course, then, sets up mysteries, problems, as-yet-unresolved difficulties with which students will wrestle all term. Narrative is also driven by turns, transformations, moments of recognition. Every good course stacks the deck in favor of these developments, even as it remembers that they're for the students to find, not for us to "deliver."[9]

It's important to say that thinking this way about the classroom isn't: a) giving up your responsibility as a teacher, or b) somehow turning the class over to those who expect you to teach. If we're trying to *induce* student learning rather than deliver teaching, we'll initially have made *more* work for ourselves, while our students will probably have roughly the same quantity of work to do but in a different register and with different consequences. The kind of work we're talking about for you is intellectual work, above all—figuring out just *how* somebody who doesn't yet understand what good work looks like in your discipline would build the curiosity, technique, habits, and understanding necessary to do that work. That it's about what *they* do becomes still more clear when you consider the point philosophically. (Note to self: Don't even think of teaching unless you're ready to think philosophically about what you do—at least sometimes.) People learn far more by doing things than by watching others do things. If we accept that this is true, then it quickly becomes clear that a syllabus isn't primarily a shopping list or manifesto: It's a design for student work.

[9] *Deliver* is, unfortunately, a verb in common use in administrative and accreditation discourse. A 2019 Open University "Innovation Report" even suggests, as an important future direction for higher education, "drone-based learning," which implies the "delivery of education" is following Amazon perhaps a bit more closely than most of us would find comfortable.

We achieve really good design only when we go through a *design process*. For most of us, that process will take place primarily in writing, so we want to state emphatically that the kind of syllabus we're advocating here is one that we arrive at through a writing process. Like student papers dashed off at the last minute, dashed-off syllabi usually aren't very good. We need the space of note-taking, drafting, revising, and rewriting to figure out *what we really think* about how our course ought to proceed.

The paradigm of "writing to learn" has spread to many departments in many colleges, primarily through Writing Across the Curriculum initiatives. In essence, it argues that students shouldn't be asked to write only to show that they've learned something. The act of writing—especially in low-stakes forms that won't be graded, like short response papers, rough drafts, or note-taking—offers students a chance to compose their thinking, figure out what they don't know, attempt to explain things they're just beginning to understand, and frame problems in terms that make sense to them individually.

So why don't we talk about the syllabus as an occasion of "writing to learn" for teachers? Think of all the mysteries of a semester—why one student disappears, why another who had seemed so promising ultimately failed, why the assignment you thought would work so well resulted in unreadable papers, and why the other one you dashed off led to such a great discussion. To come to a better understanding of these complexities, we need to write about them. In order to work through the vast terrain of what we *could* assign—all the readings, the exams, the problem sets, the presentations—we teachers need to write. Just as in the case of an article we're drafting, much of what we write won't wind up in the syllabus. Our writing process should take as its epistemic base—its foundational assumption about knowledge—the sense data of every class taught, the evidence of every assignment evaluated, and the rich resource of your scholarly life, which is itself a continual practice rather than some set of unchanging precepts.

Thinking of the syllabus as a space for understanding your teaching practice will, if we're being honest, make it harder to write it. There is no easy teaching. Ever. This is simply the hard-won, deeply felt truth of the classroom. Teaching well—with what some will call enthusiasm, some will call joy, and still others will call passion—is serious labor. If a syllabus is to enable real learning, the command not just of a body of knowledge but of the methods and ethos that underlie that knowledge, we'll have to think a great deal more about teaching. We all know the barriers to that—the privileging of research for those on the tenure track, the overworked and underpaid status of those not, the cyclical and potentially repetitive grind all teachers face. But to teach really well and to enjoy it, we ought to see teaching as one of the highest possible forms of our intellectual work, not as something separate from the core of our scholarly lives but as its animating force. Whatever we do, we do for those who come after us—and teaching is a central way that our knowledge becomes active in the world.

The Pedagogical Contract

The syllabus is also the place to think hard about questions at the core of higher learning. Or even about the idea of questions. As Jill Lepore suggests in *These Truths*, her ambitious history of the United States, the nation was founded on an epistemological question masquerading as a statement of fact.[10] In one draft of the Declaration of Independence, Thomas

---

[10]Jill Lepore, *These Truths: A History of the United States* (New York: W. W. Norton, 2018).

Jefferson suggested that "we hold these truths"—"political equality, natural rights, and the sovereignty of the people"—"to be sacred & undeniable."[11] But Benjamin Franklin made a critical edit, changing "sacred & undeniable" to "self-evident."[12] By doing so, he shifted Jefferson's claim from the surety of theology to the evidence-based reasoning of the Enlightenment.

Lepore urges us to think of the statement as more of a question: "Does American history prove these truths, or does it belie them?"[13] And, alongside this question, we're forced to ask how a diverse group of people can collectively evaluate bodies of evidence and deliberate their way to shared understandings— of real situations, problems, and the right courses of action in a democracy.

Today we are in the midst of a set of epistemic crises. New information technologies have, on the surface, democratized knowledge, but they have also enabled the mass dissemination of misinformation and outright lies. Those conditions have given rise to distrust of experts and expert knowledge, especially knowledge produced by universities. There is a widespread passive acceptance of a political economic ideology that regards knowledge as worth preserving or producing only insofar as it is capable of turning a profit for someone, which then spurs a turn toward quantification, where everything must be measured and therefore measurable. These trends have generated a profound disembodiment of knowledge, so that it no longer exists in physical and corporeal sites—libraries, archives, people, and crucially *in the social relations among individuals.*

The U.S. Constitution engages some of the ways that democratic subjects discover, evaluate, and reason about evidence, but it has produced rules governing these epistemic practices

[11] Jefferson, quoted in Lepore, xiv.
[12] Lepore, xv.
[13] Ibid.

in only certain areas of public life, primarily the law. It leaves room for all sorts of interpretation, the consideration of all manner of evidence, in everyday life—for better and for worse. People are free to reason their way to a belief that the Earth is flat. A syllabus, in contrast, *must* make rules about epistemic practice. In fact, that is its most important function and the underlying motivation for its content. *This is the evidence we will consider. This is how we will consider it. These are the ground rules for how we will work collectively through it.* The rights and responsibilities a syllabus sets for knowledge-making ultimately matter far more than those it sets for attendance and grading.

How a syllabus might do that is one of the central through-lines of this book. Always underlying that throughline is our anxiety that something has gone dramatically wrong in public use of the forms of evidence and interpretation necessary to the everyday conduct of civil society. The classroom models the world at the same time that students explore that world. As our lives are rendered more abstract, distant, and digital, it can be easy to forget just how much of a college course is made out of the everyday dynamics of each class meeting.

Teachers teach and learners learn not just out of their brains but out of their bodies. They do so because they have no choice (who ever has a choice not to be anchored in their own body?). In the classroom, the teacher's objective is the students' minds. "I'm here to help you expand your minds," says the teacher, sounding for a moment just a little bit pharmacological. But the students' minds are anchored in their bodies, just as the teacher's mind is. Teaching may be primarily an intellectual exercise, but it's deeply and inevitably grounded in the corporeal. "We educate minds," a teacher may say, but those minds are housed in bodies.

Bodies produce the syllabus, too. Teachers teach—from their knowledge, their training, from the unfinished business of their own curiosity, from the desire to inform and to create in their students a hunger for more knowledge—one might even say a desire to create a hunger for the hunger itself. The tree of knowledge is not unrelated to other addictive flora.

To bring our students—the real students of the twenty-first century—into the epistemic practices of our disciplines will require a different sort of social contract than that upon which most twentieth-century classrooms relied. As we try to ensure that we're educating a more representative cross section of the country, as our classrooms come to look more like the nation as a whole, we discover blind spots that are partly ours, partly the heritage of our institutions. The syllabus is the beginning of learning to see what had been invisible, just as much or more for us as for our students. In this way and others, teaching is a social act that cannot be automated or "rationalized"— in Max Weber's sense of the word, meaning rendered "efficient"—quantified, bureaucratized, altogether uprooted from the human realities that have always defined teaching and learning.

Which is why this book might best be thought of as a design manual, a writing guide, or simply a series of provocations. We're not here to tell you how to teach but rather to help you use the activity of composing a syllabus to discern and foreground your own questions and concerns about your students' learning.

All of this, we hope, suggests why we wanted to write a book about the syllabus and why we hope you'll want to read one. The classroom isn't the only space for learning; taking account of a full life well led, it may not even be the most important space. The college classroom, however, has long been seen as an important gateway into adult life. It would be an insult to our ideas of equality and fairness if the current push to make it available to as many people as possible also sees its higher ambitions dimmed. The classroom is only one of a lifetime's opportunities to learn, but it's a space where students can see how highly developed (and potentially narrow) disciplinary practices connect to so much else in life. The space we—teachers, students—share is an experiment, a community, and only secondarily a test, even if there are, as there almost always must be, tests, attendance records, and a syllabus.

The practices we'll outline in this book are rooted in the college classroom, but we believe they could easily echo in the faculty lounges of specialized high schools, religious institutions, vocational programs, and even corporate training units—any educational environment that makes visible a plan for what a course will do. The making-visible is the work of what usually gets called a course description or announcement, which fills something like the function of an abstract, pulling to the surface the briefest narrative of what will happen in a course. And yet, anyone who's ever taken a class knows that the real real of a class isn't going to be in a course description. It's going to be in the syllabus.

This book is written for teachers. We hang out a welcome sign to others, too—administrators, librarians, archivists, parents, anyone with an interest in education—but the book is always about teachers and teaching. And because it's about teachers and teaching, it's about students. Not about students *also* but about students *all the time.*

If we slow down that idea, it might read like this: Everything that we want to happen in—and because of—the classroom experience is to be valued to the extent that students do, make, engage, resist, embrace (ideas, histories, principles, theories—you'll know best what you're teaching and what overriding objectives motivate you). If *their* doing, making, engaging, resisting, and embracing becomes the objective of *your* teaching, then everything changes.

Which is where the syllabus comes in.

2

Turning the Classroom into a Community

If the classroom is to be a productive group, what's your job? How can you use your course's founding document—the syllabus—to bring your individual students together to learn as a group?

A college classroom is, like the modern nation-state, an invented thing that's come to seem inevitable. And like the modern nation-state, the structures that hold the classroom in place are also the structures that hold us back from seeing what it is.

Those of us who complete a university degree typically spend seventeen years as students—first in primary and secondary school, and then in college, where we gather among a group of people roughly our age under a series of authority figures. Many of us have experienced that strange moment when we graduate only to discover that the rest of life isn't organized into semesters, doesn't come to a pause every few months, doesn't tell us "good job, now let's move on to the next challenge!" Different from grade school though it may be, the college classroom is far more like all other classrooms than it is like most things *not the classroom*. As teachers, we face the challenge of working within a very, very established form, yet with an eye to preparing our students for other forms, including citizenship, after our time with them, and their time with other students, is up.

Because it's so easy for our students to take the class for granted *as a form*, they will often come to us without an active awareness of their part in making a good class good or a bad class bad. The class just *is*, and if it's not especially inspiring, then it must be the professor's fault or maybe the fault of the material.

The economics of higher education have made this challenge only more difficult. In our neoliberal moment, we all face the risk of having an unhappy student scrutinizing the perceived cost of a course (in dollars, energy, and time, all of which could have been spent on other things). No teacher wants the classroom to be the place of a fiscal transaction. Don't we all have more important goals that center on learning?

Once upon a not too distant historical time, American higher education aimed to be exactly that—higher—and if not higher for everyone, at least higher for those admitted. At the Enlightenment moment that saw, among other major events, the founding of the United States, colleges and universities were perceived as key institutions for inventing and disseminating republican virtue.[1] While they weren't the egalitarian institutions many of us now hope they'll become, they were focused on the notion that a successful democracy—at the time anything but assured—would require an educated citizenry.

Forming a new nation-state is hard. Forming a classroom of diverse students into a coherent community, if a problem

---

[1] Colleges "perceived themselves, and were perceived by the new states, as having an indispensable role to play in forming republican citizens for the new nation. . . . [The founders of the United States] knew, in theory at least, that the survival of republics depended on the *virtue* of their citizens—the capacity of individuals to put the public good—the *res publica*—above their personal interests." See Roger L. Geiger, *The History of American Higher Education: Learning and Culture from the Founding to World War II* (Princeton, NJ: Princeton University Press, 2015), 90.

on a less grand scale, is similarly challenging, or challengingly similar, especially if the students aren't ready to see the classroom that way. A syllabus isn't a declaration of the rights of woman or a constitution for the establishment of a new republic, but it, too, is an experimental document with social and political force.

We might call the syllabus—with a nod to Rousseau—a pedagogical contract. It establishes the requirements for citizenship in the community of the classroom, setting out rights and obligations, specifying times, locations, and materials, and establishing the standards of knowledge-making that will define the student-citizen's participation in a functioning social entity. We would argue that students become students not at the moment that they register for a program but when they sign on—at least psychologically—to the pedagogical contract that is the syllabus and to the little world that the classroom represents.[2]

Let's look at another classroom thought experiment. It's the first day of class, again. You and your students read through the syllabus together, with that usual nervous energy coursing through the room. You offer a preview of the material, week by week, explain the grading policy, and try to give them a sense of the work ahead. Of course, they haven't done any reading for today, much less any homework, so you'll let them go early with the first assignment in hand, as soon as you've done a little exercise in which they'll introduce themselves to one another.

Not bad, but did the introductions really move your class toward community, toward their acceptance of the pedagogical contract? What would have?

[2]Benedict Anderson wasn't thinking of the college classroom in his famous study *Imagined Communities*, but much of what he suggests about nations applies to colleges as well: They're groups that believe themselves into a unity.

Take two. Your students are getting settled in as you go through your class roster to see who's here. This time, you follow the plan you laid out in your syllabus for Day 1. That plan simply reads "Not-knowing." You may put that confession in your students' copy, or you may put it just in the version of the syllabus for your eyes only. Before doing anything else, you show them a short paragraph from the reading for next week. It's a difficult paragraph, dense with the language and ideas of your field, the field you hope they'll come to love too.

You tell them that they *have* to identify three things in the paragraph that they don't understand. You give them five minutes for this. You then tell them that now they must *name* why they don't understand each of these three things and, further, try to write down a plan for the work they would need to do to approach understanding. "John Locke's labor theory of value? What do you think you need to know to understand it?" Hands slowly rise. "The language. It's weird, old." Check. "Who John Locke is and why he wrote this." Check. "Who got to own property at that time." Check.

The questions begin with their unfamiliarity not with the idea but with the language itself and its historical moment—the texture within which the idea comes to us. Why would somebody write this? What was John Locke's point? Wasn't there a king? (Yes.) Were there slaves? (Complicated question, but yes.) The discussion might move this way, from the first difficult encounter with late seventeenth-century prose to what came even earlier—ideas of monarchy, hierarchies, and ownership. History, James Joyce has Stephen Daedalus say, is a nightmare from which he is trying to awake. For twenty-first-century students, history can be everything that happened before they were born, flattened into a vast jumble of unsorted facts and periods. Teaching nearly always involves showing students how to make the Great Flatness of the past into something with contours and perspectives—still strange, but organizable—and then helping them see the difference that makes.

You started by breaking the students up into small groups and letting them discuss what they need to know to understand the passage. Ten minutes later you bring them back to a committee of the whole—they're the same people but now with new questions. You want them to be *understanders*. It's tempting to see in the word the burden of "standing under" something and bearing its weight (Shakespeare even plays on this).[3] But building that understanding is going to require mental muscle and continuous training.

You've flushed out questions and difficulties, maybe even resentments and frustrations (you can work with all of these), and you've taught something about how thinking in your discipline works (in the case of Locke, that might be any of several fields). How will your syllabus look different to students after such an activity?

Your course isn't just about a subject—it's about learning, which means in the first instance students actively constructing their not-knowing, actively building an archive of questions, actively engaging one another under your guidance.

Learning "the material" or "the subject" can, of course, be approached through traditional, fact-based protocols and the drill of repetition. Sometimes that's right, as anyone who has wearily drilled students in verb conjugations knows too well. Or learning can be built up from students' questions and difficulties, and—most important—their interactions with one another, in response to the material, held together by your guidance and oversight. It might even be possible to teach verb conjugations that way.

[3] "Why, stand-under: and under-stand is all one." *The Two Gentlemen of Verona*, 2.5.

Students and Sovereigns

If a classroom isn't a kingdom, what sort of classroom organization can we have where the head isn't that kind of head? Where the leader isn't the boss?

Few teachers aspire to a classroom monarchy. That kind of teaching ignores the independence of students, who can refuse to participate in the classroom's work. Nothing—not even momentary chaos—is quite so difficult as a room from which all the energy has been sucked through boredom and fatigue. That, however, is the danger when the teacher fails to recognize the independence of students.

At least since Locke, whose antiquated language puzzled students a few paragraphs back, Western political thought has emphatically declared that one cannot give up one's own autonomous self, that we're each fully who we are and entitled, always, to be that person.[4] The kind of teaching we're advocating for depends upon activating that kind of faith in self: Not only are students *not* subjects of a sovereign teacher, but the students *can't not be* autonomous. Building a classroom community requires exactly that—acknowledging that the structures of teaching aren't top-down as much as up, across, down, across, and on and on, a matrix of energies that creates a social organization and that lets learning happen.

Community is a fine thing, but can the teacher still be in charge without being sovereign? You are, after all, assigned responsibility—given duties by your institution. Can you execute this responsibility without being "in charge"?

---

[4]Locke is a complicated figure in the history of ideas and the history of slavery. Although Rousseau called him "the wise Locke," the English philosopher, who famously invested in the slave-trading operations of the Royal Africa Company, seems not to have extended his foundational insight into the rest of his working life.

We think you can, and that you can do it best if sovereignty itself were replaced by a concept of distributed agency, in which one of the teacher's goals is precisely to reinforce the individual autonomy of each student. That obligation sits on top of all of the teacher's other obligations and responsibilities. Effective teaching would, in other words, depend on exactly the Enlightenment goal of liberating the individual while binding each person to the task of caring for the unalienable self.

Being a student-citizen, a member of this classroom community, is different from simply being a student. You don't need a class to study a subject, but what is often called independent study becomes a very different form of learning. A community of student-citizens is a group within which every individual has given up something (but not everything) so that new energies can be generated, new lines of communication and understanding can be made live. Communities, then, are based on collectivity, which means that they're based on trust—trust that everyone will do their share (students will read, do the work, prepare for class, engage; teachers will read, do the work, prepare for class, engage) and then depend on that same commitment from others.

In a book on how individuals come to feel rooted within a place and a group, bell hooks suggests that "communities of care are sustained by rituals of regard."[5] But, in telling the story of her mother's memory loss later in life, hooks acknowledges that sustaining these communities means we can't rely on a single, unchanging set of precepts; "new rituals of regard are needed" all the time, she writes. We craft ways for students to share ideas with one another, but that sharing depends on who's in the room each term. We encourage them to address their comments to the class as a whole rather than to the

[5] bell hooks, *Belonging: A Culture of Place* (New York: Routledge, 2008), 229.

teacher alone, but sometimes they need to say something to us, directly.

To be part of that classroom community, students give up the security of knowing firmly, performing perfectly, being always right. Teachers do, too—nothing is easier than lecturing, and nothing is harder than real teaching. When teachers and students trust one another to learn together, it becomes possible to see that a community isn't just one big thing (much less one big hug) but a lot of small engagements that can, to an outside observer, look like the chaos the teacher most fears.

Both community and classroom work happen in many shapes. Two students working together, or three, or four, delving into a problem you've posed, aren't turning from the community. They're adding to it. They're no less part of the classroom community when they turn back to the full group and take a moment at the blackboard to present what they've worked through. Even a member of the class who is working by herself isn't undoing the work of community, just as long as you, the teacher, make it possible for that student's discoveries to be shared with others. You want them sharing what they've made, what they've discovered or been troubled by, what they now see, maybe for the first time, as a problem that needs more thought. These are the kinds of tasks to which the classroom community dedicates its efforts, almost as if it were the intellectual version of a town meeting, its participants working through what needs to get done.

Some student-citizens require a bit more from the teacher. No doubt you've been to faculty development workshops or heard other teachers talking about techniques for "getting the whole class involved." The discourse of higher ed overflows with talk of being inclusive—how to be inclusive, why it's good to be inclusive. What that really means, of course, is that one must be actively aware of the danger of being exclusionary in any way. Some teachers comply (the discourse of compliance automatically comes with a sigh) as a way of satisfying the edicts of Human Resources or, more generously, as a way of putting one's teaching theory into teaching practice: I'm here for you, collectively and individually.

Then there is the matter of students who need what other students do not. Your institution may require that you include a statement concerning accommodation, the student-specific, needs-based alterations to the normal pattern of things that will make it possible for everyone in your class to be engaged participants. Most institutions permit students to declare their needs and to request what are often quite small accommodations (extra time on testing and the delivery of written work). As experienced teachers know and beginning teachers soon learn, accommodation doesn't stop with accessibility issues for students who use wheelchairs or transcription technologies. More often, accommodation is about students who identify as having what may often seem to the teacher (but not to the student) small difficulties in cognitive processing or other inflections of personality that may slow the student down. Again, we're always adapting our rituals of regard to the shape of a new community.

Many students simply need to know that they *can* make use of these allowances, at which point they can do the work at the same speed as any other student. An accommodation granted can dispel anxieties that might otherwise produce real problems. Either way, you provide these variations on classroom process so that the student can do the work as ably as possible, without the burden of a perceived weakness or failure. Your syllabus may even acknowledge students requesting accommodation, with a friendly but firm requirement that those students come to see you immediately after the first class.

A pedagogy of inclusiveness, however, aims not to distinguish types and classes of individuals but aims to be unremarkable—to not single out the student who requests accommodation, and to ensure that every student is equally a citizen of this learning community. That's where good teaching comes in: using the syllabus to make sure every student's right to full classroom citizenship is secure.

The common classifications of students in need of accommodation or special attention can sometimes fail the quiet student. This raises the question of students signaling their participation in the classroom community. How can we know if a student has accepted the role of classroom citizen if the student is not instinctively outgoing or hesitates to speak for other reasons? There are lots of ways to develop that energy among students, but too often we hear only about those built around the idea of avoiding silence. A typical activity might involve posing a difficult question (one with many possible answers) and asking each student to speak in turn. Or organizing group presentations in which every student must speak. Or keeping a tally of who has spoken and who has not. When we demand that students speak, we run the risk of focusing on the wrong thing, worrying over "participation" rather than the form that participation takes and its quality. Listening to a student's silence can be another, and especially generous, form of accommodating what distinguishes that student from the next.

Silence and speech, free or compulsory: We're pausing on these questions because they get at the heart of classroom community. A good syllabus creates the conditions in which speaking, writing, experimenting—whatever the work of your class may be—become a natural outgrowth of a student's membership in that community. It is, as we'll repeat again and again, about what they do. But it's also about how they do it, and how they do it with and among others.

However broadly or narrowly understood at your institution and in your classroom, the matter of student accommodation is merely one attempt to ensure that everyone in the room (even a virtual room) is as fully present as possible. Student presence operates within a complicated dynamic, as energy moves from them to you, from you to them. But a community of students is more than, and different from, a *collection* of students. Even if you know each student's name—and let's admit that learning names can be difficult—even if you've happily adapted to each accommodation request, building a classroom community is more. From the small seminar to the largest lecture arena, a classroom community depends on the energies that can flow *among* students, not merely the connections between you and the individual student, or even between you and the room full of students taken as a whole.

Classroom Composition

What would happen if we worked backward from imagining the best version of the very real, everyday interactions that make up class time? What could we design and signal that would encourage and enable this best, most inclusive, most active classroom to come into being? How do we ensure all our students have a voice?

That question points to the politics—with a very, very small *p*—of classroom teaching. Like citizens of the state, citizens of the classroom listen and watch for the experiences of those around them. Our goal is to help students become the kind of citizens (of the classroom, of the state) who understand the whole package of behaviors and attitudes that permit everyone around them to feel recognized and respected, even in serious and sometimes contentious intellectual spaces.[6] To

[6] It was once possible to call that package of behaviors and attitudes "the social graces," a term that hid too many assumptions.

make classroom citizenship, in other words, unremarkable, ordinary—the condition that makes full participation just what students do, because they want to. We might want to think of voice here in both its metaphorical sense—having a say and the power to say it—and its literal sense—to make meaningful noise.

Experienced teachers tend to become more comfortable—or at least more familiar—with silence, with its many types and the many ways we can hear it. There's the silence of dissidence, when a student stops showing up. There's the silence borne of student anxiety ("What if I'm wrong?"). There's the silence of the rest of the room as one student speaks *too much*, throwing off the delicate social balance that makes a class session hum with productive energy. And there's the silence of students trying to get out of the way so that others can speak. There's the silence of students working— writing to themselves in preparation for speaking soon, or completing quizzes, or rereading. There's your own attentive silence as you wait for students to speak or *while they speak* in groups.

There's even your own withholding silence. Have you ever sat back and refused to speak? Refused, that is, to co-opt the community but instead compelled students to enact it? "I'm really curious about what you'll say about this week's reading," you say, "so I'm going to shut up and sit here silently for the next ten minutes, at a minimum, no matter what."

And there are the interstitial silences that necessarily punctuate discussion. John Cage, musician and philosopher, defined rhythm as "the relationships of lengths of time," a radically open-ended conception of rhythm that could (and, in Cage's case, did) give us some pretty strange dance music.[7]

---

[7] John Cage, *Silence: Lectures and Writings* (Middletown, CT: Wesleyan University Press, 1973), 64.

The music and dance of community *is* often strange, until it's familiar. Silences, sometimes even the long, awkward ones, are a necessary part of the music of our classrooms, defining its rhythm. But it's a sometimes uncomfortable job to conduct our students toward the more sonorous and compelling silences that accompany learning. We want sound from our students, even if the sound can sometimes feel like noise. Students have all sorts of reasons for not speaking in class, and simply giving them more opportunities to speak, or—worse—demanding that they do so, is usually ineffective. You've probably felt as much. After all, some students are shy, some are operating in a second or third language, some are unprepared because of a difficult family situation or because they had to work late at their job the night before. Being "inclusive," in such cases, might actually mean *not* expecting these students to speak. It might also demonstrate that you're "listening" through their silence to what's not being said. That's difficult, and it's part of the teacher's job.

The best contemporary work on teaching endlessly reaffirms the value of student-centered pedagogy. What happens if we double down on that value? What if student-student-centered pedagogy were a thing? Not as a stratagem for offloading the teacher's responsibility to the course and the class, but as a philosophy underlining the essential work of students—most of whose classroom thinking is done in partnership with other students? Learning sounds like this, too, as communities are built two persons at a time, sometimes three—rather than in an instantaneous, collective agreement, the way it might happen in the final moments of a Hollywood comedy when the resistant outsider caves and sees the benefit of a group hug.

Communities aren't just physical gatherings—they've got an acoustic, too: noise, sound, questions, counterarguments, even sometimes laughter or the sharp intake of breath that signals complete surprise. We'll explore these sounds in greater depth in chapter 7.

Finding the Center

When a student reads your syllabus, she might see all the things she could do wrong, all the work she'll have to complete, and worry about how taking this course will affect her GPA. She's in it alone, looking out for herself. A great syllabus does something different. It initiates for her a new set of relationships—with her peers, with you, and with the ideas and arguments of countless others who will enter your classroom through readings, images, designs, and theories.

Let's just replay that point: A great syllabus invites students to try on new identities as members of a community of practice in a specific field.[8] It's not exactly a theatrical role, but it's something akin to it: an idea-space in which students try out, and try on, concepts, histories, challenges, experiments— all the things that teaching and learning involve.

The great syllabus also acknowledges that students are already members of other communities. And so it gives them the language and concepts they need to sound and think like a member of *this* intellectual community, too.

It gives them the strategies and methods they need to work like one, the social and cultural mores they need to act like one, the reason, motivation, and zeal to want to be one. It gives them the rights and responsibilities to affect that community

[8] Jean Lave and Etienne Wenger, who gave us the term *community of practice*, have much to say about identity and knowledge, though their focus is often on the world after college. See Wenger's *Communities of Practice: Learning, Meaning and Identity* (Cambridge: Cambridge University Press, 1998), and Lave and Wenger's *Situated Learning: Legitimate Peripheral Participation* (Cambridge: Cambridge University Press, 1991).

in meaningful ways. And still it holds out for them space to remain within other communities. It also implies respect for those other communities.[9] Students are part of many communities—as are you.

A great syllabus can do many things, but it does not try to *convert* students, luring them to (a new disciplinary) god. It invites them into yet one more community. An analogy from anthropology might help here.

In *Debt: The First 5,000 Years*, David Graeber describes a study by Laura Bohannan of the social customs of a rural Nigerian Tiv community. Bohannan had received gifts from neighbors—"two ears corn, one vegetable marrow, one chicken, five tomatoes, one handful peanuts"—but didn't know what the appropriate response was.[10] Eventually, she discovered that

> one should bring something back of approximately the same value. One could even bring money—there was nothing inappropriate in that—provided . . . above all, that one did not bring the exact cost of the eggs. It had to be either a bit more or a bit less. To bring back nothing at all would be to cast oneself as an exploiter or a parasite. To bring back an exact equivalent would be to suggest that one no longer wishes to have anything to do with a neighbor.[11]

And so the women of this village, Graeber writes, "might spend a good part of the day walking for miles to distant homesteads to return a handful of okra or a tiny bit of change . . . and in doing so, they were continually creating

---

[9]Of course, the syllabus can't do all of this on first reading or through being read alone. It is *always* a question of your design *in action* over the term. If the syllabus is a plan, then there has to be action equal to the plan.

[10]Quoted in David Graeber, *Debt: The First 5,000 Years* (Brooklyn: Melville House, 2011), 104.

[11]Ibid., 105.

their society." Communities are made, not born. Even the communities into which we're born are made, not born.

The classroom is a space where we are constantly giving and receiving—questions, answers, ideas, problem sets, essays, exams, professorial and peer feedback, conversation, pieces of a group report, and, yes, grades. But what keeps these exchanges from becoming mere transactions? What prevents a classroom from turning into a market where the students are customers and the professor is a service employee? And how do students learn the customs associated with exchange in this new disciplinary space?

These are not economic exchanges, but social ones. Graeber and Bohannan's analysis of Tiv customs suggests how a community can successfully avoid the tit-for-tat thinking that can drain the humanity from the giving and taking that makes up our everyday lives. In classroom relationships, there must always be a sense that there's *something more* coming, that the exchange is unfulfilled, incomplete, because there is *always a next exchange* that somehow hinges upon this one. And the underlying ethos of this body of exchanges, the rhyme and reason of them, is the need to build and maintain a community where, at the beginning of a semester, there was none, and to maintain that community via the practices of your discipline, via its rituals of regard. A class cannot work as a society—a learning society hoping to become a learned society—when students and teachers are looking for each moment of exchange to work out evenly, or worse, to get the upper hand. To put it economically, a penny-pinching student or teacher can ruin a term.

Can students learn to see their work—for you, for and with their peers—as acts of generosity, as the opportunity to give a gift and a way to build a community? Can you learn to see your work for the students the same way? Can you learn to teach your students that a community is itself an act of generosity?

In the best classes we've had as teachers, our students came prepared, were excited about the course, and spoke generously with one another—that's student-student-centered pedagogy at work—and with us. Something special happened that doesn't happen in every section. What was it? We often fall back on dumb luck: We had a couple of talented students who didn't merely do the work well. They brought everyone else along with them, because they knew how and how much to talk, when to show off, and when to take a back seat. And we had a good, broad, motivated middle range of students, the type who can work their way up to the high B or even A range if they put in a genuine effort.

The strongest voices in your classroom, yours and those of the most vocal students, will set *community standards*. That term is usually associated with the right and wrong of social formations—the playground, the neighborhood—but it's also a valuable way to conceptualize what happens in the classroom, and who decides what's acceptable and what isn't. Most students are surprisingly adaptable and will conform to whatever emerging social order surrounds them.

The Classroom Community as a Working Community

Whatever else it is, the classroom is a work-space, and a good syllabus makes plans for that work. Students are unlikely to discover this on their own. A wise professor once said that she'd discovered why one of her most talented students was continually handing in B– work. "It's because she's trying to get an A!" This little teaching koan can always remind us of the problem of getting students oriented toward a genuine engagement with material rather than meeting standards for the sake of meeting standards.

We often unwittingly frame a semester's work in terms that feel impersonal or transactional, like we're writing a policy brief rather than *writing to our students*. Our syllabi do, in fact, have multiple audiences, from deans and colleagues to the public (if they're posted online). But our students are the primary audience, and such subtleties as word choice or even whether we address them in more colloquial or familiar language can make a big difference. Our sections on grading might say something about what we think grades mean and don't mean. Our reading lists might show our own excitement for the material and our genuine interest in students discovering their own fascinations within it. Our academic honesty policies might say that we *trust* our students and expect the best from them because we respect them. We'll discuss these things in detail later in the book.

We need to communicate our own genuine motivation if we want similar motivation from them. Doing that is as complicated as any attempt to inspire others. Doing that is also as simple as talking with your students about what gets you up in the morning to teach this material, why it's important in itself, and why it's important to you. Nothing motivates like enthusiasm, which is what we call "belief plus energy"—the two qualities without which no teacher will be successful, no matter how good the syllabus.

This is why data science research like the Open Syllabus Project—a massive online collection of English-language syllabi—gives us a fascinating resource but is also prone to misrepresenting or at least distracting us from the most important business of a syllabus: communicating *with students*. Analyzing the syllabus in terms of data points can lead to pretty absurd rankings: Shakespeare is the most assigned author across the Open Syllabus Project's six million syllabi; textbook authors like Elaine Marieb or Gregory Mankiw chart in the top twenty-five. And while it might be fruitful to scan across a corpus for words denoting required skills or learning outcomes, to do so slices away nearly all of the context that matters.

To put it another way, we risk focusing too much on the syllabus as what J. L. Austin called an *illocutionary act*—a speech act that is *itself* the performance of an action.[12] The classic example is a promise: The statement "I promise to teach you the basic principles of fluid dynamics" is itself the action it describes. But a syllabus does something else—is almost entirely about something else—that can't be captured with such tools: what Austin called the *perlocutionary act*, the things that the listener (or in this case the reader) will do in response to the syllabus's locutions and illocutions. Pedagogical contracts can't, by definition, be unilateral. Students aren't *acted upon* by the syllabus. They're the people who will act *with* the syllabus.

When we're successful in shifting students toward motivated work, the classroom dynamic changes. Students who are completing assignments out of fear of failure or merely to fulfill requirements will show up to class grudgingly. When you try to turn them toward group work of any sort, including everyday discussion, they will likely be stubborn, and this stubborn dislike of the activity will set the tone for their interactions. Your class can turn into something like watercooler conversation at a bad job. Similarly, when students either aren't getting work done or are doing it half-heartedly, any sort of in-class activity that hinges on their sharing or developing that work won't go well.

[12] J. L. Austin, *How to Do Things with Words* (Oxford: Oxford University Press, 1962).

Motivated students are more likely to get their work done on time. And they're more likely to be invested in what you and other members of the class have to say about one another's work, about the course's content, and even about their everyday lives. They're more likely to enjoy spending time with one another in your class.

To get students to find motivation and to be motivated *together* requires that we consider the different backgrounds of the people in the room as a topic of serious intellectual weight. The administrative language and logic of "classroom diversity" and "inclusive pedagogy" often skim the surface of the real complexities of everyday classroom teaching. It's not enough merely to acknowledge the different experiences our students bring into class. Those differences affect not so much *how* students learn as how students *relate* to what they learn and even what that learning means.[13]

One way to get at this is by considering areas of scholarship we might think of as theoretical. Theory implies a body of largely abstract knowledge that explains how more concrete, material things work. Scientific theories in biology and botany suggest the operational principles for why animals and plants change over time. Economic theories attempt to explain why discrete transactions or financial behaviors happen the way they do. Theories in cinema studies try to account for the hidden logic (or illogic) of how films represent the world.

---

[13] bell hooks is, of course, helpful again here: "Even those professors who embrace the tenets of critical pedagogy (many of whom are white and male) still conduct their classrooms in a manner that only reinforces bourgeois models of decorum. At the same time, the subject matter taught in such classes might reflect professorial awareness of intellectual perspectives that critique domination, that emphasize an understanding of the politics of difference, of race, class, gender, even though classroom dynamics remain conventional, business as usual." *Teaching to Transgress: Education as the Practice of Freedom* (New York: Routledge, 1994), 180.

When we read theoretical writing, we often have to make sense of it largely by plugging in concrete case studies to see how a theory works and what it "really means." We read Kwame Anthony Appiah writing about national identity, for example, and we try his theory out with our own lived experience of being American or Korean or Ghanaian. We may try it out with identities not our own via stories our friends have told us (which ultimately means, again, via our own experience). You will have your own experiences, your own examples, your own connections. The point here is that we tend to understand abstraction through concretion.

The abstract and theoretical—and the possibility of exclusionary teaching—hides in unexpected places. Even when we're not asking our students to read theory, they come to terms with course materials through what they know. A microeconomics course may presume that students are familiar with what a mortgage is, even though some of them have spent their whole lives in communities where everyone rents. A business management course may provide case studies that presume familiarity with everyday experiences of white-collar workers. And it's not just that less privileged students will have difficulty imagining material associated with more privileged settings. The problem operates the other way, too: An upper-middle-class white student coming from the suburbs may find a story by Viet Thanh Nguyen "unrelatable" or inaccessible.

This obvious point—that everybody interprets everything through what they know—ought to complicate how we think about our role in building a classroom community. Let's be more intellectually serious and frame the question beyond classroom "participation." It's actually an epistemological question: How do I take the many types of knowledge and ways of knowing that students bring into my class and create the conditions in which we can learn together?

That complexity is why we're enthusiastic about fore-grounding the problem itself—using the fact of students not knowing something as a way to create a theory of teaching. Imagine a sequence of writing prompts woven into the early part of your syllabus that lead students to discover both the richness and the limits of their own experiences as those experiences relate to a current topic. What is the central argument of the text you've been assigned? What have you seen in your life that connects to that argument? Can you imagine other experiences that might frame the argument differently? Now, what does that difference—between how your and others' prior knowledge and knowledge practices shape your relationship to course material—imply about the nature of this type of intellectual work? Invite students to share their perspectives and insights and weave them into a way of talking about how experience complicates knowledge production.

You might also want, when possible, to introduce case studies and objects of analysis (concrete things) that are likely to be unfamiliar to everyone in the room. This is a way of making class an "away game" for every student—a space where no group has a competitive advantage. One way to do this is to engage in historical rather than cultural displacement: Let's look at this thing from the eighteenth century, even if our class is explicitly about our own moment, because the theoretical and conceptual questions we're asking will operate back there just as well as up here. Moving "away" will mean something different for every teacher and every discipline, but it's a useful pedagogical strategy not only in terms of community building but also in terms of one of our central motivations as teachers: to make the strange familiar and the familiar strange, to shake a student away from easy assumptions and toward the harder work of learning how to understand.

True Believers

Shaping what happens in the classroom is entirely the teacher's responsibility, but entirely dependent on the collective will of everyone in the room, a collective will that the teacher can only encourage but never command. This is the dance of pedagogy, moving through ideas, with questions, in and out of texts, across the spaces opened up by the unpredictable encounter of student and material. To do that, though, a community has to feel, and to be, authentic.

All that we've discussed so far connects to the thorny question of "authenticity." There are few more highly charged terms in modern higher ed. In 1970, the literary critic Lionel Trilling gave the Charles Eliot Norton Lectures at Harvard on the subject "Sincerity and Authenticity." Trilling traced out a shift from an eighteenth-century ideal of being sincere, with an emphasis on moral force, to a more modern idea of being "authentic"—true, real, capable of recognizing oneself and sustaining the self one recognizes. That modern sense of the authentic self has taken a lot of abuse. We've come to a point where "authenticity" has become almost entirely a marketing term.

Teachers are skeptical of the things that come out of the mouths of the development office or the public relations department. But we still have to pause and remember how to take authenticity seriously, because community is impossible in the absence of unaffected, genuine goodwill. If most of the room isn't in earnest, none of what follows will matter. How can one *will* the room into authenticity? The obvious place to start is the matter of your own authenticity.

You can't teach what you don't believe. That means not that you must believe in what a particular text says but in the importance of thinking about what the text says. Students know when the professor is wasting time, and nothing is as big a waste of time as teaching material that doesn't strike a chord with the teacher. True, this is easier to avoid when you're the one choosing the material than when you're told you'll be teaching this text or that, but the authenticity of classroom engagement has to begin with a belief in the course and its materials. For this moment, it's worth recovering, in the word *professor*, its original sense of professing belief. Teachers are believers first, instructors second.

So why does one person seem authentic while another doesn't? We've all seen prepackaged video presentations. No one who really cares about teaching students will imagine the goal to be a slick, faultless, unidirectional performance by the professor. The evidence increasingly suggests that the high-production-value online lectures some universities have produced don't work—if one assumes, of course, that the goal is student learning.

People teach in different ways. They can communicate the authenticity of their engagement, and the authenticity of the course's questions, in different ways, too. Inevitably, the larger the class the greater the challenge in creating a classroom community. But even in a darkened five-hundred-seat lecture hall, it's possible to convey an authentic engagement with the material and—even more important—an authentic engagement with the importance of teaching it.

A class of normal size—lights on, students visible and nameable—offers so much more. Here's where your students can see you, not just as an authority but as someone real who wants to be with them. Students know when you want to be in the classroom, and if you don't want to be there, community won't happen. Authenticity is visible in your openness to their ideas, in your mentioning something you read in the news that morning that connects to the material under consideration that day. It's a cliché to suggest that when teachers show their passion for their subject, students notice and want to show up. Like some clichés, it's also true.

And yet you know that teaching is also a performance, and that sometimes you *don't* want to be with your students. In your syllabus and in your classroom, you aren't presenting your "true self" (as a student might perhaps put it). It's something else, neither false nor exactly, perfectly true. Much as your students aren't the same people in your class as they are with their parents at home or their friends in the dorms late at night, you can't (and shouldn't) be your private self with them. You're some other self, engaged in what we might think of as the "genuine theatrics" of teaching. There's nothing synthetic or false about inhabiting the role of teacher. In fact, it can become more possible to do it well when you think of it as a kind of theatrical performance. Tone matters tremendously. Again, start from how you understand someone else to be genuine. Body language is important, as are the kinds of things the person is saying, especially the questions, the feeling, the belief.

This tension between authenticity and performance exists both for you and for your students. If we return to the question of the experiences that students bring with them into the classroom, then we can start to see what a classroom community really requires. Your students are who they are, with their markers of identity and their preexisting knowledge intact, but they're performing a particular version of themselves just as you are.

It may not be going too far to suggest that many of our social and political problems at present stem from a collective failure to recognize this tension between authenticity and performance—and the different ways it's complicated for different people.

How can we practice inclusivity while also teaching students how to perform the work of our disciplines? How can we welcome the students, as they really are, when we know that implicit in the act of teaching is the prospect of our students' transformation into some new form of themselves?

It would be too easy to say, defensively, that in bringing a *polis* into being, a syllabus does not espouse any particular political ideology. That's not entirely true. While most of us are horrified by the image of the college classroom as a space for political indoctrination of any kind, we do in fact argue for particular forms of rationalism and reason that are, in a broader sense, political.

So when we craft a syllabus, let's choose to think actively about the plan we're making for students to know together and how to know together. The modern nation-state has a long way to go before it can achieve the kind of community that you and your students can build in a small room, with little more than a blackboard, good lighting, and the gift of one another's full attention.

3

Clock and Calendar

A syllabus disciplines the time you'll spend together. Every syllabus lays out the work of a course in a linear progression of assignments. But how do you and your students really experience time when you're living out its design?

"Time's up. Pencils down." The spot quiz is over. You steer attention back to today's material. A hand goes up. Instinctively, you look at your watch. "A good question—but we don't have time for it just now."

It was a good question, too, but it took the class away from the material you had to cover before the bell rings, which it does, as bells do. You continue, looking down at the notes you didn't get to, as your students gather their things. Other students are already at the door, ready to nab the best seats for the class that follows yours. There are six more weeks to the semester. You're calculating just how far behind schedule you are.

In most classes, the syllabus can feel like a giant time-keeper—for the students, for the teacher—ticking off weeks until midterm and then finals. How many clocks do you need to tell time in a course? The semester, the length of the class session, the pacing of assignments, in-class activities, student presentations. All can feel as if they impose constraints on the syllabus and what the teacher needs to get through, as if time were a constant threat, a many-headed, single-minded hydra with yet more creative ways of keeping the teacher from teaching.

Can you build a syllabus that understands time? Maybe. But first you'll need to give yourself the freedom to understand what time means for the community that is your class. The astrophysicist Stephen Hawking wrote *A Brief History of Time*, explaining to nonscientists nothing less than how time works in the cosmos. This chapter merely aims to explain how time works in a classroom.

We've already raised the idea of the syllabus as a pedagogical contract with the student, a promise that material can and will be taught, though it will happen successfully only if the student fulfills a series of paced obligations and clears formal hurdles at specific points. We have a lot of names for those obligations—attendance, readings, assignments, class presentations—and the formal hurdles are, of course, exams and papers.

The syllabus is also a contract involving temporal obligations. Such and such will happen at this point, and it will be followed by the next episode, and that one by another, and all the while the clock will tick.

As any teacher knows, it's more complicated than that. Reading a syllabus is a bit like reading the summary of a play, scene by scene, in which you can imagine what will take place in live performance and how long it might take to do it, but without the full script, much less the sense of the theater's precious transience. Among the things that make theater so powerful is its impermanence, its gone-in-a-flash presence, the reinvention of a moment so that its effect is a lot more than the minutes it takes to happen. Even if you've taught the course before, the syllabus can't guarantee that the moments you hope might galvanize your class will, in fact, do just that. The syllabus is a timekeeper, but it's also a lot of other things, too.

Two Kinds of Time

The Greeks had two important words for time—*chronos*, what we think of as chronological time (it's there in *chronology*, the report of events as they occurred in sequence), and *kairos*, or the moment, the opportunity, the well-timed thing that happens, usually because someone does something. *Chronos* goes on whether we like it or not. *Kairos*, on the other hand, is a chance, and you either take a chance and seize the moment, or you don't. The nick of time, we call it. In her translation of Sophocles's *Antigone*, a play about, among other things, decisions, actions, and being too late, the poet and classicist Anne Carson seized the chance to help us see the distinction between *chronos* and *kairos*. She calls her version *Antigonick* (the cover of the New Directions edition helpfully spaces the title's letters—ANTIGO NICK—to make the point even clearer). Who acts in the nick of time? Who doesn't? The truism that life happens when you're doing other things has its counterpart here. *Chronos* plus *kairos*: Time is really time times two.

The syllabus has its own *chronos*. Time goes on. A good syllabus is full of *kairos*, too (it's a noun, so the plural is *kairoi*). In designing it, you've set up the places, events, exercises, questions where something can happen. A great syllabus understands that there are lots of ways in which to think about time, about *chronos* and *kairos*. You might be teaching a class chronologically, with each element in one continuous historical line. Or you might be teaching in shorter chronological arcs, returning in each unit to an earlier point in time, as you might in a comparative history of the development of the nation-state. Or you might deliberately disrupt chronology to concentrate, say, on formal properties in the development of hand tools across cultures.

If you teach, you know instinctively that what you do has variations in rhythm, tone, difficulty, emphasis. You might be a teacher who tries hard to iron those functions out—an evenness of tone, a uniformity of difficulty—or a teacher who makes the variations become a source of the class's energy. You might be a teacher who, over the course of the semester, crafts a series of problems that increase in difficulty and depend on the practice of a series of skills.

However you structure your material, and lay it out week by week, you're looking for *opportunities*—those temporal junctures where something special can happen. Those pedagogical nicks of time are there for the seizing. As a teacher, you can plant critical events in the material, moments so obviously important that every student will know to pay special attention, a bit like the crucial events in act three of a Shakespearean tragedy. (Remember learning about turning points in a play?) Some teachers are brilliant performers, able to divide the hour lecture into acts, with built-in tensions and surprises. We admire—envy, even—that skill. But the *kairos* of the active classroom isn't something you can script, the way you cleverly orchestrate the critical moment in your lecture on the fall of Hanoi or the invention of the spinning jenny.

There's little as gratifying for a teacher as the moment when the student "gets it"—makes a connection and pulls seemingly disparate strands of ideas into focus. It may be important for you, as a teacher who is also sometimes a preacher and almost always also a performer, to have moments in which you craft a connection and show your students how two ideas fit together. But that's different from the moment when your students can seize the material and make of it something of their own, on their own, by the force of their own insight. A good *kairos* is always an opportunity. You can lead your students to it, but it's there for their seizing.

Of course, if that's true about *kairos*, it's possible only within the *chronos*—the remorseless clock time of the course. The syllabus imposes a time constraint, just as a train schedule does or an egg timer is built to do. The train schedule tells you when you will arrive and the stops you'll make in getting there. The egg timer tells you when the job is finished, reminding you that if you were to go longer, you'd ruin it. We have to live with semesters, because that's the unit of delivery for most educational institutions, and most teachers are happy for the limitation that the end of the semester brings. So why not the syllabus, too? Like the semester, the syllabus encapsulates the limits of what can be done within a given period. Its temporality is unlike any other, so let's give it its own name: *coursetime*.

Coursetime

In coursetime, there is always more to do than space permits, always more possibilities, always more avenues to explore. A Hollywood comedy from the 1960s about Americans touring Europe was called *If It's Tuesday, This Must Be Belgium*. It's easy for an overpacked syllabus to send off a similar signal: If it's Week 3, This Must Be the Industrial Revolution or a similarly modest subject. In coursetime, great subjects are often crammed into small spaces, and syllabi groan under the weight of the teacher's ambition or obligation for the class.

Large lecture classes, especially in introductory courses, are frequently committed to the idea of *coverage*, a concept that has been under attack now for decades. For some teachers, coverage means a chronological survey of a topic or period, within which the levels of detail, the selection of primary and secondary readings, and the shaping narrative of the lecture bind the subject into a coherently deliverable whole. For other teachers, coverage is an old-fashioned, even quaint idea, lacking an up-to-date pedagogy necessary to engage the concerns and questions most urgently affecting students' lives. Coverage has come to feel more actuarial than pedagogical, more like what your insurance policy is about than the syllabus for a course.

In the smaller classroom, where teaching and learning more effectively take place, the question of coverage can become overwhelming. A desire to be sure nothing important is left out of a syllabus leads easily to syllabus bloat, which in turn has important consequences, not only for the student but also for the learning community of the classroom.

Anyone who has been through college knows what syllabus bloat looks like. But looked at from the perspective of coursetime, syllabus bloat becomes especially worrisome. This book tries to set its marker down on the experience of real people in real classrooms. That isn't meant to squelch the idealism that makes the best realities of the classroom possible. The syllabus is always an idealized, imaginary vision of a subject—or rather an idealized, imagined vision of the best questions to ask about a subject, accompanied by the best tools with which to ask those questions. That's a lot of idealism, all of which has to be delivered in practical terms.

Every syllabus—however ambitious and scrupulously planned—exists in coursetime. The most effective syllabus makes choices—many kinds of choices—in order to make the best use of that coursetime. Different classroom settings and different educational levels, as well as different teaching environments, will determine how much must and can be covered by a syllabus.

Sometimes it can feel that not every teacher is given the same clock, as if the differences in teaching environments or educational levels were different brands of a familiar product.

And, of course, different educational settings—the places where teachers teach the students in those places—*do* in fact constrain teachers and courses in different ways. High school teachers, subject to state and community requirements, will build or follow a syllabus that may leave little room to question the idea of—or even the ethics of—coverage.

At the university level, the syllabus for a graduate seminar, which is centrally dependent on the full, preprofessional commitment of the students around the table, may recommend much more reading than can possibly be discussed in the seminar's coursetime. A graduate seminar often operates on the principle of a banquet: The students are given an immense laboratory of ingredients, from which they develop their own inventions and bring them to be shared and tested. Some are derivative, some undercooked, and most of the best are in need of a lot more work. Reading and talking about this work shapes a graduate school's coursetime.

Someone teaching an undergraduate course, however, can depend on a much tighter set of temporal controls. The semester is still no longer or shorter than for a graduate class, but the students are busy in very different ways. What happens in and around their classroom occupies a smaller portion of their lives. The Carnegie Commission's recommendation on assignments and class prep—that the work required of a student outside a class should take twice as many hours as the class meets—can come as a shock, both to student and to teacher. The student enrolled in a three-credit class asks: "You mean we're expected to spend six hours reading the textbook?" No, but in this three-credit, three-hour class you're expected to spend six hours working through all the parts of your obligation—doing the assigned reading, preparing to discuss intelligently whatever questions the teacher has asked the class to consider, working on your paper, conducting research, and so on—all of which will quickly fill six hours. Or the teacher asks: "You mean I have to have them read only half the novel, because it would take more than six hours?" No, but if you've assigned Dickens's *Great Expectations*, and your own great expectations are that the students will read the whole novel, you'll have to come to grips with the fact that a five-hundred-plus-page book will take much more than six hours to read. It's not just a literature course problem. Think dense—and not even necessarily long—readings in econometrics or analytic philosophy.

Students aren't afraid of work. Most are serious about their studies, even in required classes. But their clocks are complicated, multilayered affairs, just as yours is. Students expect the syllabus to recognize the demands placed on them by other coursework and, more often than not, by their lives outside of class. Work, family obligations, long commutes, athletics, arts programs, apprenticeships, volunteer projects, and other standard complications of college life would seem to have little to do with the work of the classroom. But they all shape the student's experience of coursetime, which can easily move from prime time to whatever time is left. How can your syllabus recognize the way students navigate coursetime?

In practical terms, the syllabus isn't one big, demanding clock. It's a lot of little clocks, whirring away, sometimes oblivious of one another. Consider some of the clocks the teacher needs to think about in constructing the syllabus for any course. The clock of the strictly mandated syllabus will require something like a mechanical adherence to form and time-keeping. Central to a successful syllabus, and to a successful class, is its pacing:

the pacing of readings
the pacing of assignments
the pacing of review and return of student work

How much students can and will read is knowable only once a class is already underway, so teachers have to work from their experience or the experience of others at their institution. The pacing of assignments—the number, length, and due dates—needs to be calibrated in relation to the work done in the classroom.

Students are smart. They will know when an assignment is make-work and when it responds in a meaningful way to the work of the classroom. That, in turn, obligates the teacher to construct assignments that are responsive to coursework and to the students themselves, whose engagement and interests may lag behind or race far beyond expectations.

A syllabus may repeat itself, like a sorcerer's incantation, from year to year, but students don't. Each class is different; each group reinvents what the same syllabus means. The pacing of assignments also sets a corresponding obligation upon the teacher, whose task it is to see that the work is reviewed and evaluated. This may be a matter of correcting calculations or observational procedures, as in a lab report, or reading with care a student's paper and providing written feedback. In larger classes, this work may be off-loaded onto teaching assistants, a familiar organizational structure that disperses labor without lessening responsibility. Big lecture or intimate seminar, what's essential is that the work be returned to the student as quickly as possible.

Coursetime can and should incorporate feedback. But feedback can take many forms. There's no reason that it all has to come from the teacher, though of course the teacher's feedback may be the voice the students most want to hear, at least until the students get to hear their own voices engaging with other students' work. There are many ways you can ask students to develop a practice of self and peer evaluation, something we'll think more about in chapters 5 and 6. Assignments might have their fifteen minutes of fame at the beginning of a class, with the teacher setting the criteria by which students should critique the work. Their judgments can become a part of the class discussion. This type of feedback—a rewiring of the traditional one-way communication of teacher to student—can dramatically change your students' perceptions of time. Where your comments, editing, and marking up on student work can easily disappear into the black hole of a backpack, strategically deployed peer-to-peer or student-to-self feedback can slow students down and make them notice the quality of their work. Students listening to other students is teachers seeing their own work in action.

This is a moment to say that the syllabus is (danger: another metaphor ahead) also a kind of garden where you do a lot of planting. Not just ideas but the real possibility for student agency. Agency, not control. Do this right, and you lose nothing as a teacher. In fact, it works the other way. The more students can exercise their agency—their informed, active, sometimes noisy work with you, and with one another, but in your presence—the more you've made the classroom the learning community you want it to be. That's where the garden metaphor comes in. Leave space in the planting bed for growth. Seedlings don't sit still. Something as simple as "Student peer work today" declares an objective. Or it can be a note you keep on your own copy of your syllabus, a practice we'll consider at greater length in chapter 8. You say: "I didn't tell you I would do this, but instead of collecting your response papers I'm going to have you do peer work on them. I'll only see the next version—the one you'll turn in next week that should reflect what you've learned from other students today." Try it.

As Cathy N. Davidson reminds us in *Now You See It*, "research indicates that, at every age level, people take their writing more seriously when it will be evaluated by peers than when it is to be judged by teachers."[1] And not just writing, but student *work*. Which means that one of the goals of teaching is to make it possible for students to think outside the box of their own writing, to deploy that critical generosity that makes it possible to comment usefully on another student's writing.

The overarching principle is simple: Keep it active, and keep it together. Since the work of the course is a continuum always in danger of breaking, the community of the classroom depends on everyone understanding what coursetime is, what needs to get done by what points in the semester, and why. That commitment—taking seriously the obligations laid out in the syllabus—falls on both students and teacher.

Both.

Those teachers who complain about students handing in late work might ask themselves whether they return graded work quickly and no later than promised. The two clocks are related. The time between turning work in and receiving it back is rapidly expanding time, a space in which the student's engagement with the assignment is most likely to escape, like precious helium from a necessary balloon. It's also a matter of what used to be called—simply—setting a good example or, more recently and more technocratically, best practice. If you want students to believe that their work must be done on time, you'll want to show them that you can do it too. It's one of the clearest demonstrations that both teacher and student live in the same coursetime, working under the same clock.

As you might say to your students: Write this down. We sometimes, and sometimes justifiably, allow ourselves to delay handing back student work when our other teaching obligations overwhelm us. But students can't and shouldn't know

[1]Cathy N. Davidson, *Now You See It: How the Brain Science of Attention Will Transform the Way We Live, Work, and Learn* (New York: Viking, 2011), 101.

this. There are so many ways in which the classroom is like theater, and this is another. The exchange of work from student to teacher, from teacher to student is a kind of dialogue—a teaching dialogue, if you like, but one in which there are not only two speakers but two listeners, waiting for what the other has to say, waiting for what the other person hears. In the classroom, work is conversation just as much as it's clearing hurdles. It would be a strange, experimental play if the characters onstage never responded to one another—or only did so after three or four weeks.

The well-timed syllabus knows this about the classroom community. At least the teacher's own copy of the syllabus should include not only the dates when assignments are due but the dates when graded work will be returned. The corollary to this principle is that, if possible, you'll want to build assignments into your syllabus that you can turn around quickly—steps in a process, short but revealing opportunities to assess where your students (and you) are in the work of the course.

Fundamental to the structure of any course, and to the syllabus that charts it, is this idea of direct correlation: Assignment becomes graded work, or at least work returned promptly with a response. Similarly, the work of reading—the assigned chapters, documents, or analyses that the syllabus says are required for Week 2—needs to be incorporated into the classroom work of Week 2.

The teacher may believe that the syllabus is the trail of bread crumbs through the complexities of the subject, but it's rarely so straightforward. For many teachers, this is hard-won knowledge: The course has met for only one week, the teacher has reminded the class of the readings, laid out in the syllabus, for the following week. When that week comes, and the readings are not, in fact, discussed, the class has learned one of the most powerful *negative* lessons: Suddenly, the syllabus looks like a series of suggestions rather than requirements, and it may be unnecessary to complete the specified readings for the specified class meetings. This is one of the open secrets of successful teaching: If you assign it, use it.[2] If you're not going to use it, don't make your students read it. And by the way, if you're not going to use it, think again about why you would put it on the syllabus at all.

The most important clock-and-calendar events for most courses will be the final (whether a written exam, a demonstration or presentation, some sort of paper, or a critique) and, sometimes, a midterm exam. In some institutions, final exam weeks add a dedicated slice of temporality explicitly for the purpose of organizing finals. In other institutions, finals are part of the regular class-session schedule, as midterms usually are. Designing a syllabus with an eye on several clocks means making space for these exams, as well as any other you may require. A course that opens every week with a pop quiz on the week's reading may gain the attention and grudging respect of the students but at the cost of time that otherwise could be used for learning. Only you will know what's right for your class. Whatever you decide, both you and your students will still be living in coursetime, with its own complicated dynamic.

The constraints on the time available to the teacher not only limit what can be taught in the available weeks but also can determine the methods by which the material can be taught. Can I take the students to the university library's rare book room? the soil analysis laboratory? downtown to the art museum? Maybe, but that affects the flow of coursetime.

---

[2] The nostrum "use it or lose it" is eminently applicable here, though the first *it* is the reading you've assigned, and the second *it* is your students' enthusiasm for the class.

Off-Season

Coursetime flows in only one direction, but it flows unevenly. The first weeks of the term seem to go slowly (there's all the rest of the semester ahead) but also rapidly, crowded with student conferences, dropping and adding, and the exhilaration of new ventures. Student work is likely to arrive more or less on time, especially if the teacher has emphasized the importance of the syllabus's schedule and has demonstrated that work will be returned quickly enough for the student to think through what worked and what didn't.

As the semester flows on, however, the shape of coursetime may undergo a curvature worthy of Einsteinian physics. The teacher notices that student work arrives later and later, assigned readings are engaged hastily or not at all, and the presence of other courses being taken by the students suddenly looms large, as if the teacher's course were suddenly subject to a powerful gravitational surge.

Seasonal change only exacerbates the problem: In the fall, when the Northern Hemisphere's days grow shorter and temperatures drop, the approach of winter is blamed for adding pressure on a student's ability to concentrate and complete work. In spring, when days finally begin to lengthen, it's spring break and then the promise of summer that can mock the carefully designed syllabus, with its season-neutral confidence in higher things. By April, students are tired. Their teachers are, too. Semesters that run well into June face SAD—not seasonal affective disorder but summer academic dysfunction.

Summer months, have their own touchingly optimistic clocks, crowded with the belief in the possibility of simultaneous leisure and productivity. In theory, summer is the stretch of time when students work jobs and teachers do research, write, prepare new courses, and refresh old ones. Summertime is a conceptual marker for off-the-clock leisure, warmth, and rest. We all love summertime.

Summer *time*, however, is something quite different. Some programs are designed so that summer is a crucial period for course work. Many teachers teach a summer term in order to make ends meet. If the concept of coursetime extends into the summer months, it becomes especially bendy.

Consider the ways in which summer coursetime is different from academic-year coursetime. When you're teaching or studying, and everyone else you know isn't, you might feel either virtuous or put upon. In either case, your sense of time is constrained by the unusual circumstance of summer study. If you really did need the summer off (as a teacher or as a student), you may be coming to the task already anticipating late-summer exhaustion before a return to the "real" academic year.

A semester's work has to be translated into a small span, usually anywhere from a maximum of eight weeks down to a punishingly intense three (yes, that sentence deliberately avoids "compressed"). Imagine a month of gym training in which you have a rigorous set of exercises that your coach sensibly spaces out so that your muscle groups have the opportunity to absorb the strain you've put on them, giving you enough rest time to rebuild tissue. Now imagine your coach decides you don't need the rest time, that there's too much to do, and all your muscle groups will be worked to the max each day. It won't be long before an aggressive training program meets somatic reality. The body can only do what the body can do.

A three-week version of a fifteen-week semester can run similar risks. It's not difficult to schedule the same number of contact hours (say forty-five) in a three-week period. It's even conceivable to require that the student will spend twice that studying (that's the Carnegie guidelines again): fifteen contact hours and thirty study hours a week for three weeks. Theoretically, one three-credit course plotted out over three weeks should be something like a short-term, full-time job. But the body and the mind work in tandem, and the work of thinking—imagining, absorbing, reflecting, challenging, inventing, making big mistakes, making small discoveries—requires a lot of coursetime. You can pile on the work and satisfy state and institutional requirements, but it's more difficult to leave the student the space to think.

The syllabus—any syllabus—says much about a course, but it rarely says, "Think here." Summer coursetime offers little think-time. What you can do in eight, much less three weeks, is very different from what you might do in a fifteen-week semester. The teacher's time, as well as the students' time, is simply different than in a standard term, and a syllabus has to reflect this difference. It shows itself in the way students are expected to read, to reflect, to produce work. It shows itself in the ways the teacher is expected to present materials and ideas, respond to and evaluate student work, and create a classroom where concepts and arguments, histories, and theories need to be reinforced daily instead of weekly. As a consequence, the intensive-session syllabus has to be different from the full-semester syllabus, if only because learning is reflective, and not merely absorptive. That means that students—and teacher—need good old-fashioned somatic time to get through the work.

There are many ways in which to think about the shape of a semester and the means for responding to it effectively. In a sixteen-week semester with four major assignments, do you have to space those work units four weeks apart? Can you front-load written work so that students have more time for other assignments later in the term? Alternatively, can you learn more about what your students are learning by getting work back from them very early in the semester? If the syllabus spaces assignments unevenly but with a purpose, does that "create" time you can use for review sessions before the exam, final paper, or concluding project?

It's not more work. It's different work. Or rather, it's work distributed creatively across coursetime so that students can get the most out of a course. Even exhausted students want to succeed.

The constraints of the syllabus are about time, among other things, but that shouldn't be discouraging. The creative syllabus finds fresh and inspiring ways to understand the course's subject and the most pressing questions that arise from or may be applied to that subject. The sufficiently extensive syllabus doesn't lock itself into an idea of coverage, finding instead an alternative that's ambitious and teachable. As for the lives of students, every teacher has the choice of imagining either an audience of theoretical listeners or real people with whom a learning community is co-built.

The syllabus inhabits a whole set of time constraints, and it's easy to feel that the class is bound in by, and tied down to, an unreasonable set of limitations. But teaching involves the engaged passing of time with students who are studying ideas and the urgent in-the-moment time that is hard to plan. That's the *chronos* and *kairos* of teaching, the spooling out of ideas over a semester and the spontaneous thrill when a student responds with clarity and freshness to what another student has, with equal clarity and freshness, just said. If you've had that experience, you may have said to yourself, with a private grin, "My work's done here," because there and then the class was doing the work of teaching itself. But we know that such moments are rare, which is why we treasure them and why we go on teaching, always hoping that another *kairos* may happen, when the student has an epiphany and the room is suddenly electric with understanding.

The *kairos* may be the classroom's rare and special moment, but *chronos* has a lot going for it. One of the things we may not talk enough about is the timeliness—the well-timedness—of teaching. Think of the minutes necessary for students to "get it" by "taking the time" over an idea, an argument, an assignment. Timeliness, too, in the sense of raising a point or a text or an experimental procedure exactly where it needs to occur. Successful teaching acknowledges that the body and the mind want time to absorb concepts and questions. Recognizing that is recognizing coursetime.

The syllabus, like the semester for which it stands, is time-bound and timely. Things happen in time, because there's no other way for them to happen, and they build across the span of the course—as if there were a dramatic arc—from some place to another place.

At a simple level, the other place is always the end of the term, when you're administering that final exam or collecting that final paper. But the semester that preceded that moment won't be evenly available to your students' recollection. Daniel Kahneman casts doubt on a conception of time and memory in which an "experiencing self" is "simply the sum of the values of its moments."

> This is not how the mind represents episodes. The remembering self . . . also tells stories and makes choices, and neither the stories nor the choices properly represent time. In storytelling mode, an episode is represented by a few critical moments, especially the beginning, the peak, and the end."[3]

What are the critical moments your students will aggregate to construct a story of the course? We can't always anticipate

---

[3] Daniel Kahneman, *Thinking, Fast and Slow* (New York: Farrar, Straus and Giroux, 2013), 406–7.

what they'll be, but we have to try. We'll keep thinking about the nuances of storytelling in coming chapters.

So the classroom feels like a clock, and in many ways it is. The syllabus is always there, beating time, and it can feel, too, as if the syllabus is beating you the teacher as well as your students. But the syllabus is also the structuring device, the mechanism that frees the teacher to move the discussion forward, to advance the students' thinking and problem solving as they move from unit to unit. That only happens, to be sure, if the syllabus marks out a path sprinkled with opportunities for invention and discovery—the chance to seize an idea, maybe in the nick of time, and pull it into the work the classroom community has come together to do. In the classroom, and on the syllabus, time is the indispensable enemy, the treacherous friend.

4

What's a Reading List? And What's It For?

Is the reading list a set of windows? A library? A mine? A cohort of mostly silent teaching assistants? However you build and use the reading list in your course, what do you expect it to do for—and with— your students?

"The reading list? Why it's the course!" you might say. That's why it's clearly part of your syllabus, and might be included in your department's announcement of classes before registration. Is there a better way to announce what a course is going to be than with a title and a reading list?

A reading list is both the heart that animates a course of study and the skeleton on which the course is built. Naturally, that makes it the skeleton on which the syllabus is built, too. But it's more than an armature. A reading list is also a teacher's cast of players, as well as the cache of ideas out of which you and your students will build still more ideas.

Technical courses of study most often depend on a textbook, which is a sort of reading list of one, in which the students work their way through chapters and progressive exams to establish their understanding, step by step, of complex material. A course in civil engineering, for example, might require *Mechanics of Materials* by Beer, Johnson, De Wolf, and Mazurek. It's a McGraw-Hill textbook, now in its seventh edition, and if you're not in the field you've probably never heard of it. (That, by the way, is one definition of a textbook.) If you are teaching the subject, however, *Mechanics of Materials* could be the only entry on your course's reading list. You'll expect your students to read it, chapter by chapter, in the order assigned and according to the timetable laid out in the syllabus.

But suppose you are instead teaching a course called "How to Think Like an Engineer in Society." Since you would be hard-pressed to locate a single teaching tool that did everything you needed, you diversify what you want your students to encounter. Your reading list might include several different kinds of things to read, and even things to watch or listen to. One of them might be Henry Petroski's book *To Engineer Is Human: The Role of Failure in Successful Design*, a work written by an engineer for nonspecialist readers.[1] Petroski, a teacher of engineering as well as a historian, has written about such technological wonders as the bookcase, the pencil, and the toothpick, and he knows how to write a sentence. There might be other nontechnical entries on your reading list, alongside works from contiguous disciplines—perhaps a study of how inner-city communities develop survival strategies or how immigrant populations alter the ways cities grow. These, you argue, are good things for an urban engineer to know how to think about. *How to think about.* That's not exactly learning a technical detail of construction. It's more meta-knowledge about engineering or a general view of how cities really work. That's why you're teaching the course and inventing a constellation of readings and materials to make the class possible. That's why you'll choose readings that, besides being

---

[1] Henry Petroski, *To Engineer Is Human: The Role of Failure in Successful Design* (New York: Vintage, 1982; rpt. 1992, with a new afterword by the author).

pertinent and interesting, will enable you to build the right kind of assignments.

A reading list might map a subject confidently and simply. (Psychology 101 requires the Psychology 101 textbook. End of story.) Or a reading list can just as easily announce a subject's complexity—a range of perspectives, opinions, and theories, interpretative models and counternarratives. A reading list can say a lot. It's not surprising, then, that assembling a reading list can be one of a teacher's most challenging, and invigorating, activities. And why not? Everything about a course is yet to happen. Until then, the teacher and these smart reading materials wait for students to arrive.

Not Quite a Short History of the Reading List

Where do reading lists come from, anyway? Wouldn't we love to know exactly what Plato's students were required to read? In Aristotle and other ancient writers we have tantalizing glimpses of works and writers now lost. But even if we had them, those works would be subject to two millennia of thinking about the world, including the world of these ancient texts. Medieval pedagogues, for whom the university was a new invention, operated within a restricted universe of texts and an even more restricted universe of materials and approaches with which to teach them. With the mechanical reproduction of texts and, later, with the invention of photography and other recording devices, a course of study could be structured around a more expansive and more individually inflected idea of what had to be read. That concept enters English only in Victorian times.

The *OED* traces the earliest uses of the term *reading list* to the mid-nineteenth century. Was it a bookseller's list of materials for sale, as an 1859 example would suggest? That would make it something close to a catalogue. By the 1880s, a reading list was specifically connected to a course of study. A century and a half on, the reading list is almost identical to that course of study, in which the *course* is something that moves through time and space, like a stream, or that runs its course, like a fever. In the twenty-first century, we've become used to the idea of the reading list *as* the course, *as* the syllabus, even *as* the object of study.

Even before *reading list* became a term of pedagogical art, the classroom was built around readings. Any history of education with a long view will reflect on how standard texts—from Cicero, as read in the early modern period, to the McGuffey Readers of nineteenth-century America—have shaped not only what people learned but the idea of a curriculum. For centuries, Cicero's writings on politics, friendship, and other difficult subjects were studied and imitated in Western European classrooms. In Tudor England, the Welsh mathematician Robert Recorde, an early proponent of algebra, wrote a widely influential treatise on teaching mathematics that was still in use more than a century later. (Recorde is credited with inventing the equals sign = as well as the wonderful word *zenzizenzizenzic*, meaning "to the power of eight.") The McGuffey Readers, which once taught the three Rs and now evoke a *Little House on the Prairie* nostalgia, dominated primary education in the United States for over a century. Cicero was a model to be imitated; Recorde and the McGuffey books, as different as they are, were meant to explain subjects to students who needed to learn them. Modern pedagogy doesn't depend heavily on *imitatio*, and Cicero's glory days in the classroom are past (meanwhile, we're poorer for the decline in oratory and rhetorical skills). The work of textbooks, however, has only become more sophisticated and demanding.

The modern reading list is designed to enable teaching that cannot be done by a textbook: If everything you wanted to teach in a class already existed within the covers of a book, you would assign that book and be done with it. By its existence, the reading list says that the course prizes its uniqueness. These readings, chosen by this teacher, will open up the class in unanticipated ways. Entries in a reading list are variables in an equation. The more variables, the more complex the equation, the more connections to examine, the more questions to pose and perhaps solve.[2]

So, one gets down to work in choosing materials that are right for the institution, the course level, the class size. Even the same course, taught by the same teacher in different years to different populations of students, can require adjustments to a reading list that seemed perfectly calibrated to its subject—or at least it did the first time round.

For today's teacher, imagining a reading list is a simple thing—the internet! online texts! paperbacks! photocopies!—until the headaches begin: the question of quantity, anxiety about the students' attentiveness, worry about coverage. Then there's your own relationship to reading lists. They were formative to your own education; you share reading lists with colleagues teaching the same subjects; you compose lists of readings for yourself. The more you think about what a reading list should be, the more you're likely to reflect on how you and your subject have shaped one another.

What goes into a reading list? Some instructors choose materials they know well and teach year after year, sometimes

---

[2] Many of us have had summer reading lists at one point or another, a piece of paper on which we've jotted down the five Great Books we want finally to read (Homer, Dante, Proust), all of Austen (again) or all of Morrison (again), or maybe it's a guide to soil science for gardeners or a history of contemporary Chinese art. Building a reading list this way is about the commitment to a reading project—the *list*-ness of the list can be more important than the specific titles in it.

without change. Others look for what seems like an ideal balance between tried-and-true teachable materials and experimental engagements with new readings, those that show up on a syllabus for a single semester and then, like seasonal flowers, are replaced by the new crop of promising selections. Yet other brave souls reinvent the reading list each time the course is offered. Time, life, students, experience, and disciplines all change, so why not the readings? Many instructors, many courses, many approaches. Most, however, are bound by a teaching vision based on a sequential engagement with printed materials. Love me (or my course), love my reading list. For many of us, the reading list is simply those things we will study and that the student must read.

Where does a reading list appear on a syllabus, and what difference might that make? You might, for example, announce at the end of the syllabus several important works that symbolically stand for the course itself. For a class on the individual and community in late modernity, you might choose Robert Putnam's *Bowling Alone: The Collapse and Revival of American Community* alongside Rebecca Solnit's very different *Wanderlust: A History of Walking*. Some syllabi double down on the reading list, indicating which of the works listed needs to be read when, the selections attached to specific weeks (Week 8: Putnam 183–215, Solnit 81–160), without necessarily requiring the entirety of any author's text. Some teachers resist what they think of as spoon-feeding the class by breaking the readings up this way. Others see it as a means of ensuring that the material gets read.

Teaching an entire book, slicing it into sections, and attaching those sections to specific weeks permits the teacher to focus, and not coincidentally alerts the class that the teacher really does mean that you have to have read these pages. Specific reading assignments have another advantage, too: They give the teacher the opportunity to guide the students' engagement with the author's work, here a long section of a book about the history of walking—in the country, in the city—and what we might learn from it. Sometimes the weekly reading is determined by the teacher's sense of how quickly students read. Sometimes it's determined by the ideas that organize the course.

There are pluses and minuses in the week-by-week breakdown. Reading an entire book feels like it should be the gold standard, and in many ways it's what we hope our students will want to do, devouring a text, page after page after page. That gesture reflects the mimetic model of teaching: Be like your teacher and immerse yourself. In graduate school training, which is fundamentally preprofessional, that sense of the reading list feels reasonable. Here are the books that are central to the course. Now read them. Yet graduate students are not just older undergraduates. By graduate school, the advanced student has developed strategies for reading and patterns of making sense of what has been written in a field. Handed a list of titles, graduate students are likely to know what they are looking *for* and where to look for it.

Teaching undergraduates, as well as high school students, and building a reading list for them means providing a more specific set of directions: not only what to read but how to read and what to do when you get there. The readings you identify on the syllabus tell the student what to read, but you can make the announcement of those readings do a lot more. "Next week we're going to read Putnam and Solnit, two very different writers thinking about very different perspectives on the problem of being an individual in postindustrial society. As you read these texts, this is the question you should be thinking about." You then launch the question. If you get the question right, your students come to class primed for a discussion of the texts within the larger context of the semester's work. If it's a lecture course, their informed preparation allows you to take a deeper dive into the subject.

You might object that these are questions of pedagogy and not exactly of reading lists. But the reading list isn't just the content that you teach. It's also a tool you use to teach students how to read all sorts of things, including a reading list itself.

There are famous reading lists. In the humanities, one can turn to the vertigo-inducing document that the poet W. H. Auden provided for the course he taught on "Fate and the Individual in European Literature" at the University of Michigan in the fall of 1941, a year when the fate of the individual in Europe was very much in question. Auden's reading list gestures grandly and widely (*The Divine Comedy*, Horace's *Odes*, *Moby Dick*, one drama by T. S. Eliot, four by Shakespeare, *The Brothers Karamazov*, and so on). Auden includes nine opera libretti, which he clearly thought of as important European literature, and adds a further list of recommended reading, in which he finally includes works by two women, both distinguished anthropologists.

Much has been made of Auden's list. For some, it's a bracing reminder of a time when an undergraduate would be given a mountain of treasure and expected to examine every coin and gem. The core humanities curricula at places like Columbia University and the University of Chicago keep alive the big vision of a massively ambitious undergraduate humanities education, long decried as the cemetery of dead white males and now given more dimensions by the inclusion of writing by persons not male, not white, and sometimes not even dead.

Few of us today can indulge in the vertiginous ambition of Auden's reading project. Fewer of us would want to. The aging twenty-first century is a different place—technologically, pedagogically, socially, politically—than the pre-digital American Midwest during World War II. It would also be hard to

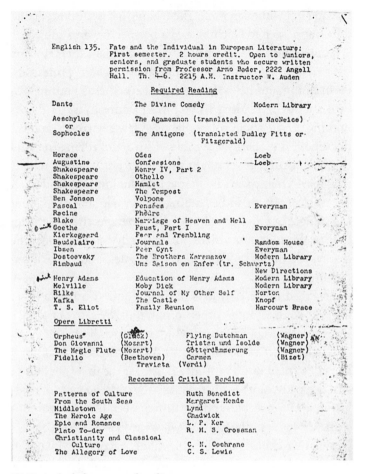

English 135. Fate and the Individual in European Literature:
First semester. 2 hours credit. Open to juniors,
seniors, and graduate students who secure written
permission from Professor Arno Bader, 2222 Angell
Hall. Th. 4-6. 2215 A.H. Instructor W. Auden

Required Reading

Dante	The Divine Comedy	Modern Library
Aeschylus or Sophocles	The Agamemnon (translated Louis MacNeice) The Antigone (translated Dudley Fitts or Fitzgerald)	
Horace	Odes	Loeb
Augustine	Confessions	Loeb
Shakespeare	Henry IV, Part 2	
Shakespeare	Othello	
Shakespeare	Hamlet	
Shakespeare	The Tempest	
Ben Jonson	Volpone	
Pascal	Pensées	Everyman
Racine	Phèdre	
Blake	Marriage of Heaven and Hell	
Goethe	Faust, Part I	Everyman
Kierkegaard	Fear and Trembling	
Baudelaire	Journals	Random House
Ibsen	Peer Gynt	Everyman
Dostoevsky	The Brothers Karamazov	Modern Library
Rimbaud	Une Saison en Enfer (tr. Schwartz)	New Directions
Henry Adams	Education of Henry Adams	Modern Library
Melville	Moby Dick	Modern Library
Rilke	Journal of My Other Self	Norton
Kafka	The Castle	Knopf
T. S. Eliot	Family Reunion	Harcourt Brace

Opera Libretti

Orpheus	(Gluck)	Flying Dutchman	(Wagner)
Don Giovanni	(Mozart)	Tristan und Isolde	(Wagner)
The Magic Flute	(Mozart)	Götterdämmerung	(Wagner)
Fidelio	(Beethoven)	Carmen	(Bizet)
		Traviata	(Verdi)

Recommended Critical Reading

Patterns of Culture	Ruth Benedict
From the South Seas	Margaret Meade
Middletown	Lynd
The Heroic Age	Chadwick
Epic and Romance	L. P. Ker
Plato To-day	R. H. S. Crossman
Christianity and Classical Culture	C. N. Cochrane
The Allegory of Love	C. S. Lewis

W. H. Auden's famous reading list.

conceive a course that by definition was uncompletable.
Because the first rule of reading lists is the saddest: Your student can't read everything, and neither can you. So we choose,
not only what is best and most important but what is most
useful for the community your classroom works to sustain.
We invest much in the selection of materials on the reading

list, and not without reason: The reading list is the poster child for an approach to teaching and a perspective on a subject.

Sometimes teachers worry about the signals their reading list may give off to others: deans, other teachers, professionals in contiguous fields. In the digital age, there's nothing private about the reading list for your course, just as there's nothing private about your syllabus. A few keystrokes, and the document is globally accessible. It's worth keeping in mind that the document we might intend for our students only is readable in many ways by many different kinds of readers. A course description and a reading list say a lot not only about the subject but also about a teacher's perspective on a field. Our reading lists are where our scholarly interests meet the discerning publics of students, colleagues, and curriculum committees.

So a reading list may look like the requirements you've set for your course, but it's other things, too. A vision of a field, a set of questions, a historical window onto a discipline. A set of possible keys to possible locks. What might it mean for a student to read Rumi or Audre Lorde for the first time? Or to struggle with Kant's idea of justice? The consequences of reading are unforeseeable, and the unforeseeability of those consequences goes to the heart of what we do as teachers.

What we choose to assign inevitably becomes evidence of a set of assumptions—yours, or maybe your department's—about a subject. We might like a reading list because it distills and codifies. "My reading list marks out the coordinates of the subject, and with it my course can lay claim to a field of inquiry." We might like a reading list because *reading the list itself* is an act of affirmation. "My reading list is a gesture, a story about a field, and a set of questions." It should be, too. For some teachers, a new course's reading list is a declaration: The problem we're studying is real and requires our attention—new approaches to marginal tax rates, environmental change and aquaculture in Caribbean nations, the psychological consequences of overcrowded prisons—even if there can yet be no exhaustive, defining statement on the subject. When a reading list is carefully coordinated to coursetime, it becomes not just a sequence of encounters with a subject but something more—a series of markers that lay out something like a story.

If your course has weekly readings—and every successful course has something for students to do for each class meeting—you'll have fifteen or sixteen chances to engage your students with voices that are not your own. A reading list is polyphonic, if only we look at it that way. Shorter readings are easier to allocate: an article, this report, that white paper—something that can and should be readable in one sitting. Anticipating what your students can consider a one-sitting reading and breaking down the weekly readings accordingly can help create the conditions for a more serious engagement with the material. Thirty pages? Fifty? Fifteen? The right number will vary from discipline to discipline, from text to text, and from course to course. Don't be reluctant to prepare your students for what the syllabus says about readings. Why have you chosen this? Assigned that? Given the Age of Infinite Technological Distraction, it's never been more important for you to take a moment and talk about the readings as central, as required, and as valuable. Then you'll need to craft your assignments to run in parallel with readings. We'll get to that in the next chapter.

Most of us compile reading lists made up of important works—classics, things that made our minds pop, trusted old friends, new discoveries. We want so much to believe that reading lists are central to the course that we can easily forget a guiding principle: Readings are windows, not monuments. Even the most encyclopedic readings are samplers, selective engagements that—to return to our metaphor—help move forward the story your course is telling.

Because stories can't tell everything and still be stories.

They leave things out for the sake of building a narrative, offering a perspective, and engaging an audience. Anyone who has ever put together a reading list knows this: By definition the list is incomplete. There is always more, always something you have to leave out, always approaches and materials missing, just as your course itself can't possibly cover every aspect of its subject, no matter how carefully you've planned it out. A syllabus—a reading list, a course—is partial, not just in the sense of being incomplete, but in the sense of directing its audience toward a way of seeing a subject. Window, not monument, at least not here, at least not now.

Homer is a monument, but teaching Homer is about giving the student tools to read Homer: That sounds circular and paradoxical, but stop and think about what you expect a student to get from reading the first two books of *The Iliad*. All sorts of things about mythology and poetry, drama and human interaction, the function of the gods that humans have built for themselves, the difference that two millennia make. Homer the monument is also a window onto Homer the monument. We put a classic like *The Iliad* on a reading list so that the six weeks our students can spend with it will throw that window open wide and let Homer in.

The same holds true in STEM courses. Your students must learn a set of equations and principles, but they are doing so in order to build a framework of knowledge—a set of interrelated ideas and approaches—that define a stage in learning the work of your field. You may recall early chemistry courses you took, when you found it difficult to compose the lab report because you never knew what your motivation was supposed to be in the first place. "A solution was formed by titrating . . . ," you wrote, obediently doing the busywork asked of you. You were saved ultimately by a teacher who sparked your curiosity and helped you understand what these seemingly rote lab experiments were really all about—you discovered your monument, and were astonished to find it was a window, too.

All of this is to say that a reading list is also incomplete in that it's just sitting there, waiting to be used. Someone's got to read the material contained within it. When you assign reading, you are obligating—or better, inviting, enabling, helping—your students to do something active and powerful. Your syllabus needs to communicate to students, in ways both subtle and overt, the need for this active commitment to the reading. Because we sometimes fail to fully imagine our students in that act of reading, our syllabi sometimes fail to create the right conditions for students to read well.

Required Reading, Recommended Reading

"How much of this is required?" asks the student. Before anything else, that question means, "Do I have to buy this?" For students, reading lists look like shopping lists, imposed by an authority on their shrinking student dollars. There's a not unreasonable backlash about the costs of required materials in college today. "Two hundred dollars for the books on the syllabus?" complain both student and parent. In some fields, that's a normal expense. In others, it produces syllabus sticker shock.

How much should required books cost? It's a difficult calculus, especially in an era when the price of college is already stratospheric. Universities spend enormous amounts of money and require it too, from families, donors, and taxpayers. What is the right amount of money to ask students to spend in your course? The answer will be different from course to course and field to field, with greater tolerance on the student's part in disciplines more visibly—let's stress that word *visibly*—connected to employment tracks than the liberal arts.[3] (The question of the cost of books is rarely reframed in terms of other college-related expenses. Do we expect students to express resistance to the costs of a necessary computer, for example, or an activities fee?) Still, the realities of the classroom are what they are. Students welcome less-expensive solutions to the cost of education, and many respond to a list of required books as a cost to be circumvented when possible. Knowing the culture of your institution, which includes student expectations of outlay for study materials, can help you earn your students' trust that you understand the real financial challenges they sometimes face.

Are your readings required, or recommended? Reading lists contain one type or the other and sometimes a combination of the two.

Required reading: what you *have to* purchase, borrow, rent, or download in order to take this class.

Recommended reading: what you *might or should* purchase, check out from the library, or download in order to deepen your knowledge if you are so motivated.

Required reading is often thought of in terms of material that must be *mastered*—a word that feels strangely out of place in twenty-first-century education. Who lives to be a master, anyway? Perhaps equally important, the idea of "mastering" material can have different senses of importance in different educational environments. We want a medical student to

---

[3] The report on the unemployability of liberal arts graduates is premature. See, for example, the Association of American Colleges and Universities 2014 report "Liberal Arts Graduates and Employment: Setting the Record Straight," https://www.aacu.org/sites/default/files/files/LEAP/nchems.pdf; and Derek Newton, "It's Not Liberal Arts and Literature Majors Who Are Most Underemployed," *Forbes*, May 31, 2018 (https://www.forbes.com/sites/dereknewton/2018/05/31/its-not-liberal-arts-and-literature-majors-who-are-most-underemployed/#52c892ee11de).

master the material in the study of hematology. We probably don't want an anthropology student to master the material in the study of a particular indigenous people in Australia, at least not in the same way. That's partly because the forms of knowledge in med school and anthropology consider the world in different, though not unrelated, terms.

Both the med student and the anthro student will, however, have required readings. These are the nonnegotiable tools with which the class will move forward. Very old pedagogical models (not so old that you haven't experienced them, though) depended on rote memorization and the repetition of what the teacher said. Today we're more likely to consider the readings not only as material to be learned but as the course's lingua franca—the common trading language—in which ideas will be exchanged. But first, we need to think—happily if we can manage it—about the virtues of the partial, the incomplete.

To the teacher, the reading list can seem straightforward. To the student, a reading list can seem a complex puzzle organized by three primary questions:

Must or could? Do I have to read it (and, if it's not freely available, buy it), or is it a strong suggestion?

All or some? Do I have to read it all or just a selection—and what selection?

When? Do I have to have read it for the dates listed on the syllabus, or will the teacher stray from the plan?

Thought of this way, the reading list becomes even more clearly a set of possibilities and challenges for the teacher. "I'd like you to read as much as you can, of as many of these as you can, and be prepared as often as you can to discuss them." That may feel cooperative, even generous, but it's a difficult instruction to put into practice.

It's easy to put a book on a reading list. It's more difficult to determine exactly how much—which really means how little—you actually need your students to read. But that's part of the art of building a reading list that works.

The reading list is there to be used by you and by your students. Regularly. Without fail. If you're not going to use something in class, be sure you know why you won't *and explain to your students what you expect of them, anyway.* If you go through that exercise with your class, even one time, you may find that you've rethought the selection entirely, either to drop it or to create some engaged activity with your students that brings the selection out from the cold and into the warm space of active learning.

Think of the reading list as a thing to be used—a set of tools or the material you'll work with using those tools, a collection of ways of seeing, a fleet of vehicles that will carry your class to a variety of destinations. Then concentrate on the ways you—and, more important, your students—will use it.

Thinking with the Incomplete

Like the national debt, our daily workloads, and both human knowledge and human error, our reading lists have a seemingly natural tendency toward growth. It typically happens this way: You're designing a class and deciding what you will teach. Your ideas are built on the work that's gone before you, the explanatory and the speculative, the historical and the theoretical, the "then" of your subject's past and the "now" of your subject's present. All aspects of your subject have a relevance to larger questions. There may also be matters of urgency, whether for public policy or geopolitical decision making or simply because a field of study is on the cusp of rediscovering what matters most.

So you bundle together the books and articles, the online video materials, and whatever else you can summon, like a magician, to do your bidding, at least for the length of the semester. With the best of intentions, you come up with a list of essentials, the readings you're convinced that your students must be exposed to before they go one step further in their education. The reading list grows, and soon there's too much. This book needs to be balanced by that book, and this set of perspectives needs the complement of another. We try to fill in gaps that we imagine exist; maybe we imagine we can fill them if only we can get our students to read yet one more thing.

So reading lists grow, but they can grow in different ways. We prune them, but that often stimulates new growth, just as it does with plants. We substitute for one entry another we think works better or is a bit easier for our students, but then we hedge and restore the original material we cut—we really did want our students to read it—to the half-life of recommended reading.

If a reading list is intended to cover a field, the teacher is committing to a breadth, historical or methodological or thematic, and selects readings that will do that. One teacher might aim for piecemeal coverage, a reading on X, a reading on Y, a reading on Z, as if the subject could be domesticated one cognitive acre at a time. Another teacher might aim for coverage by juxtaposing narratives and counter-narratives. So a history of X, a different history of X, a critique of the history of X, and so on. Coverage by adjacency, coverage by repetition, but in either case the aim is coverage, as if the subject must be proclaimed and protected at the same time. "Got you covered," says the soldier shielding a comrade in a tense moment. Sometimes the teacher sounds as if the subject of study needs protection just as much as the students need exposure to it.

Or sometimes it's less about coverage than about *copia*—the Latin concept of plenty (as in *copiousness*, or that horn of plenty, the *cornucopia*), the notion that the reading list is a groaning board of choices. The more delicious offerings the better, and as long as the quality remains high, there's no reason to limit them. You can see how Auden's view of a syllabus resonates here: Who would strike off Dostoyevsky? *Hamlet?* Kafka? The exaggerated posture of Auden's selection can make any normal, overlong reading list seem tame by comparison, but the grand sweep of Auden's list shouldn't be a blind to conceal one's own unreasonably ambitious set of readings.

The first open secret of the reading list: A long list is easier to craft than a short one. The second open secret of the reading list: Whatever the length of the reading list, it will challenge your students to engage other thinkers, and it will challenge you to teach the material, or should. One of the most common problems of teaching the same courses year after year is the danger that the reading list, like other aspects of the syllabus, will be trapped in amber: the same images in an art history survey, the same selections from the great philosophers, the same five Shakespeare plays, economics case studies, or environmental dilemmas. More than one successful teacher has felt, after three times with a syllabus, that the reading list has to change, no matter how successful the course feels in the heat of the moment, because the teacher needs to keep it fresh.

Some reading lists confront the problem of coverage and approach it from a side door. Where one reading list seems to demand that *these very texts* are the crucial readings for the subject, a different approach relies on representative texts and symptomatic engagements, which in some fields are called, simply, case studies.

In many disciplines, cases—whether they are examples, symptomatic occurrences, or paradigmatic moments—are crucial teaching tools. Law and business are only two. In a case-based syllabus, the class has the opportunity to pull apart actions, conditions, things done and written and said, assumptions and consequences, and to explore critique and analysis when not everything one might want to know can, in fact, be known. Case studies can feel artificial, but they can also help demonstrate one of the truths of becoming an informed individual and citizen: We almost always need to make decisions and judgments in situations where we would like to know more, where something is missing, where there is a gap in knowledge that we have to live with while we still think through a problem.

Each of us knows that we can't teach everything about the subject, that our treatment of it will be incomplete. And yet we don't know it. We're likely to load up the syllabus with too much required reading or recommended reading. If you do this, it may be because you think you need to show your students as much as possible about the subject. Maybe you want to shore up every important avenue the course will explore, providing your students with authoritative materials they can study, the better to appreciate your lecture or to participate in lively class discussion. Maybe you simply want them to read more than you know the course will support, that there can't possibly be enough time to talk about all this material, but it's better your students have too much than not enough.

You may not say such things to yourself, much less out loud, but some form of this thinking leads to overcrowded syllabi and demanding reading lists.

In the next chapter, we'll look at what our students can learn from the always-incompleteness of a course, when carefully crafted assignments enable them to begin to see our disciplines' gaps and elisions not just as opportunities but as the very heart of our continued scholarly and professional activity. Few teachers pretend that what they're teaching is complete. Fewer still probably say that much to their students.

Step back and look at your subject, and at your students, and you'll see that there isn't time enough in any course to do all the things even the most well-intentioned and enthusiastic teacher will want to undertake. More to the point, there's the practical fact that students won't read more than they feel they can. Some teachers might assign five hundred pages of weekly reading in a graduate seminar and a tenth of that in an entry-level undergraduate class. As we say several times in this book, you will know best what will work for your students and what won't. By any standards, however, "getting through" material is already an acknowledgment that there's a mismatch between your best teaching instincts and a sense of obligation being imposed upon you and your students.

How you will think about a course's reading list depends on many things. If your class comes with a preordained list of readings, you'll be thinking about them differently than if you are responsible for creating your course's reading program from the start. Are your required readings also required purchases, or are online versions of the materials acceptable? How important are specific editions? Are the required readings—in the sense of texts to be purchased or downloaded—the same documents that you will be discussing and studying during class meetings? Or are they fundamental background, essential but at the same time peripheral to what happens in the classroom, week after week? Are there, in other words, two implicit orders of readings for your course, even if you don't spell out a distinction quite that way?

So the reading list can try to cover a subject in many ways—through a big picture that strains toward completeness, or a series of partial windows on the same subject, or a set of primary documents or cases from which student and teacher will create the course, or some combination of all three. In practice it's never a complete anything, because no subject can be cordoned off into a discrete parcel of knowledge and safely delivered to your students. Designing a reading list is about embracing the partial, embracing the incomplete. To be able to do that and not see it as surrender is surely to achieve one of the higher planes of pedagogical enlightenment.

Making Use of Everything

Many families have a rule about Thanksgiving dinner: Nothing goes to waste. The turkey gets carved up on that overstuffed Thursday, and favorite pieces of the bird's anatomy are portioned out. Some people look forward to the comparatively stress-free day after Thanksgiving as the real, secret holiday, when the refrigerator is stocked with everything left unconsumed from the day before. Then there's day three, when the kitchen's presiding spirit may determine that whatever is left of the bird will now be turned into a soup or stretched with pasta and slid into the oven.

There's a lesson here about teaching, and maybe especially for the teacher who sees the syllabus, and the reading list within it, as a banquet, a Thanksgiving spread of ideas. The reading list is the big turkey, with lots of parts, some more immediately appealing than others, but all capable of being used in one form or another. Of course, you don't build a turkey (that's been done for you by Mother Nature), but you do build a reading list. How different does that list—and all the reading components of your syllabus—become if you think of the material as something that has to be used up? We already speak about students *digesting* the material (thank you, Francis Bacon, who in the age of Shakespeare gave us the distinction between books to be tasted and those to be chewed and digested). But what happens if we push that idea just a bit further and think about the material our students are asked to read as the course's foodstuff? For vegetarians and vegans there are other, noncarnivorous metaphors that would work here, but the principle is the same: Reading lists can be thought of as documents not merely to be used—in the sense of being referred to—but used *up*.

And that takes us, again, to *use*.

If you've read this far you'll recognize our belief that what the student attempts and accomplishes in the class—not what the teacher delivers in lectures or checks off of reading lists—is the real focus of teaching. The lectures may be crucial, the readings essential, but it's what the student does with your lectures, with the class's readings—what you've been able to help the student do with them—that's the core of your class. In other words, teaching becomes the act of leading students into and through materials and questions *and* leading students into and through what you, and others, say about materials and questions. Windows, not monuments. You teach a subject, usually by way of readings; that is, you teach how to make the readings useful tools for understanding the subject and for generating questions. Thanksgiving dinner is about eating a meal, but it's also about meals themselves.

How to Read a List, or Pretty Much Anything Else

Regardless of your field and subject, teaching becomes—among other things—teaching students *how to read*. A law student reads a document one way, a social-work student reads another way, a psychology student yet another way. A criminologist, a literary historian, a med student, a poet will all read in slightly (or broadly) different ways, informed by their disciplinary histories and professional frameworks. Imagine, for a moment, all of them reading, say, Flaubert's *Madame Bovary*. Each would pull something different from the text. Each would refract the tedium of Emma's life in different ways. Yet each would be drawn into the task of careful, attentive examination of Flaubert's word choice and narrative, using the novel's evidence to make sense—or a dozen different senses—of what drives Emma to infidelity and suicide.

Reading a novel isn't much like reading a work of political history, much less a clinical textbook or a legal brief. But all might be appropriately placed on the reading list of a syllabus for, say, an interdisciplinary course on social life in nineteenth-century France. The question we face in making those choices, in deciding what should appear as essential, is more complicated.

In recent years, there's been a lot of truly terrible thinking about the goals of education. We see schooling as an opportunity early in life to prepare students for careers, sure, but also for citizenship and personal fulfillment. At the heart of that understandable—and ambitious—desire is the belief that schools and universities can, and therefore must, teach not only skills but ways of thinking about thinking. The problems that students solve in a classroom can teach them not only about solutions but about *solving* itself. But—and this is the crucial *but*—for this to happen, the teacher always has to be looking at not only the precision of what's placed in front of the student but how that precision can scale up to larger and larger problems. Many of us teach as if we were jewelers, finding the precise angle at which to crack the stone so that light will strike it in the most brilliant way possible. It is too easy to forget that few of our students will become jewelers. The precision of engagement has to become a scalable skill, part of a set of skills that are the purpose of the course, whatever its subject.

Which is where the reading list comes in. Rule number one of readings, which we repeat here: If you put it on the syllabus, use it in class—at the earliest possible opportunity. Asking your students to read a chapter of Robert Merton's *Social Theory and Social Structure*? You've given an assignment to them—and one to yourself, too. In deciding to include Merton, you asked yourself: "How will reading Merton allow me to teach a new set of questions and problems?" "How will the students understand this reading in light of what we will have done in class up to that moment?" "How can I plan to have them work with the selection?"

Of these three big questions, the last is surely the most important. Serious teachers see the knowledge they teach as constituting something richer than mere "use value," or perhaps more accurately, they understand use value as a much more flexible, supple concept than it appears in the endless op-eds calling upon higher education to graduate people ready to meet the needs of industry.

So what about the concept of use? "How will this course help me?" "How will this help my daughter or son?" The questions aren't bad ones, at all, though many of us can feel blindsided by what seem challenges to our professional creds. To be sure, there are reasons to train in order to start and run companies or to develop the necessary tech skills to join the labor force in a particular discipline like engineering or computer science. But the best teachers in these disciplines know that the value of what the student can take from the class is couched in the same real-world, ordinary-people, globe-in-crisis problems that anyone teaching the social sciences or the arts or humanities will face. The best teachers know, that is, that they're teaching more than a single, narrow discipline.

We who teach face the daily, unending challenge of balancing our jeweler's craft and our acknowledgment of the life on the street and outside our borders, places where the jeweler's knowledge can be transformative, but only if the right questions are asked early on and continually, and the student's responses honored. We hope that in offering reading to students, it is as though we are lending an ax to those who have been trying to chop down a tree with a shovel or, in desperate cases, a butter knife. But it takes time and experience to learn to use the ax, and not a little risk—risk borne more by the new woodsperson than by the veteran chopper of trees.

Teachers who want their students to use their disciplines' tools with skill, purpose, and integrity know that love of and enthusiasm for a body of knowledge are never enough.

Students need to study materials you select, and that studying needs to take the form of them doing something with the materials, not simply ingesting them. A reading list is a display of your selections. At least for yourself, aim to articulate—out loud—what your students should get from the reading, what connections they should make, what questions they should be asking. If you're lucky and have highly motivated students, they will think of things you didn't. That's more than fine. It's terrific. But the central idea of this dynamic is that you select readings (with a purpose, as specific as you like, that you can articulate to yourself), conceive of discussion questions or assignments for that reading, schedule the discussion or assignment within the syllabus, and then make that classroom event happen.

Why do we make such a big deal about this? Because it's too easy to teach *against our students' best interests*. Assigning readings and not using them—right away—teaches students that the readings are avoidable because they are not important to *you* and therefore not important to *them*. It's a small but critical dimension of building a successful syllabus. Some teachers like the casual mode of presenting great works (whatever the field) and holding a class in thrall. It's romantic and appealing and now feels more than a little quaint. Many of us have studied with great women and men whose brilliance was balanced by an eccentric lack of enthusiasm for the structural ordering of a syllabus. (Note that the absence of a syllabus isn't a guarantee that the instructor is one of those galvanizing figures out of one's semi-mythical past, wearing Harris Tweed with leather elbow patches, sitting in a haze of cigarette smoke.) We're a nonsmoking, mainly tweed-less academy now, and our students expect us to be organized, enthusiastic, hardworking, and even fallible. The moment to pose as the great sage has passed, perhaps to be lamented but not to be missed. To that end, nothing gives the right signal more effectively than a well-plotted syllabus.

Teaching is, among other things, teaching the syllabus. Not just teaching *to* the syllabus—checking off the things listed, week by week—but teaching the syllabus itself, as a text, as a document, as a repository of questions and problems, and, ultimately, as a model of the very intellectual work we're inviting our students to perform. They almost certainly aren't ready to write their own syllabus, but they may learn enough over the course of a semester to understand why *you* wrote it the way you did and to begin to imagine other ways it could be done, other designs—intricate or elegantly minimal—that could be wrought with the tools on offer, even other tools that belong in this kit.

So we need to ask ourselves, "Why is this course looking at these issues? How can we use these readings to understand what's at stake? With limited time, and with a group of students with limited but diverse backgrounds in the subject, how can this reading list make engaged study possible?" Showing students that the reading list isn't an imposition but an inhabitable structure, a place within which to explore rather than a series of hurdles, a set of materials and documents about which one can argue: These not-so-simple goals animate a well-chosen reading list—ambitious, doable, and humbly aware that it doesn't know all the answers or even all the questions.

Nor should it. The best questions are those that arise naturally, from students who have spent time reflecting on the assigned readings and used those reflections when they tackle the assignments you craft.

5

Their Work and Why They Do It

What changes do you hope a semester's work will provoke in your students? How does your plan for the term make those changes possible—or, better, probable? What happens if the syllabus is a design for change?

Students fail assignments. And sometimes, assignments fail students.

Understanding the difference requires from us as teachers a quality of near-heroic endurance and a healthy mixture of self-doubt and self-confidence. Self-doubt because any time students are failing, we need to ask whether those failures stemmed from our assignments. Self-confidence because we do, in fact, know a lot more than our students about our disciplines.

Students fail assignments because they are distracted, overwhelmed with work in other courses, unprepared for your course, working too many hours as they try to cover rent, dealing with extracurricular challenges, or simply uninterested or indifferent. If a bored student falls asleep in a class on forestry, is the student really bored? Maybe, but it's up to us to understand more deeply what we mean when we sense that the class and the student aren't in sync. There are lots of reasons a student can be unconnected from what you're trying to do.

In contrast to these scattershot sources of student failure, assignments fail students *by design*. That is, by their nature, poor assignments induce unproductive failure. A good example is the writing prompt that looks for the student to say exactly what the teacher would have said. Of course, we nearly always construct these failing assignments with the best intentions.

So what's a good assignment, and how do we know one when we see one? It's easy to think that a good assignment is good in some independent way: artfully conceived, clearly written, neither too difficult nor too easy. But if we want to connect all the pieces of a course together, we can only really evaluate an assignment in relation to the assignments that precede it and follow it. That is, it's not enough to produce a good assignment or even a semester's worth of good assignments. The goal is to produce a *sequence* of them. Thinking pedagogically, the chronological passing of time is not a sequence, in and of itself. In a good sequence, things happen.

Good sequences of assignments minimize unproductive failure—and induce the right amount of productive failure. The good sequence of assignments is good not only because it works out a progression (of tasks, of ideas) but because it embeds students in a narrative. Faced with increasingly difficult challenges, students will, to varying degrees, overcome them and emerge transformed. The good sequence of assignments doesn't guarantee every student an A or even a B, but the well-ordered progress of tasks can leave even the C student feeling like a success.

The syllabus is your best opportunity to improve the odds that your assignments will succeed. Working from that early vantage point before the course begins, you can think about your future students' work divorced from the complex personalities and abilities they bring with them. You can focus on *the work* they are making. You do this because you are not teaching the material—you're teaching students, and the best way to do that is to start from the work you as the teacher need them to do.

Starting from the Work

Here's a thought experiment meant to help you sharpen that focus. Imagine that the content of your course—whatever material students must work with, such as equations, procedures, the content of lectures, reading, and so on—has been chosen for the single purpose of enabling and supporting the assignments that students will complete. Imagine, in other words, that you had to come up with the assignments *first*, and everything else, from lecture topics to textbooks, *afterward*. What would you need to do?

You might have any number of good reasons to object to such an approach. In the physical sciences, for example, there are concepts that appear to transcend our apprehension of them; the point is the knowledge, not a set of skills. It is also obviously true that without a body of knowledge to communicate, assignments become meaningless—they cannot, in fact, be separated from content. We aren't asking you to abandon such objections, and we aren't asking you to build a course entirely out of assignments. We are simply asking you to *pretend* to do so, for the sake of the insights you might gain. It's the thought experiment that counts.

Such a shift in thinking can reframe coursework's purpose from evaluating and ranking students' mastery of content to learning the facilities, developing the habits of mind, building the knowledge, and embodying the ethos necessary to work in your discipline. Notice the shift in the prior sentence: Those first verbs—evaluating, ranking—belong to the teacher, while the second set—learning, developing, building, embodying—belong to the student.

In this thought experiment, then, students do work in some particular order, and this order becomes the underlying narrative of your course, a narrative within which students—these students, in this class—are very much present.

Imagine the experiences of your students as they progress through the work you'll assign. It's helpful to start from the final work you hope to get from them, the thing they should be able to do at the end of the term. Whether it's a final project, an exam, or a performance, name—out loud, at least to yourself—the component activities students will need to perform to a high level in order to succeed in this final work: Doing x really means doing a, b, c, and d. Now think about how students will learn the right articulation of these activities, how they'll master each individually and in concert.

Or try to. And fail. Because *this* is the core of teaching, and it's incredibly difficult. You, the teacher, *will* fail, but you will also succeed, with any luck, at least a little, if you look at your own practice and speak with your colleagues about their practices.

When people repeat the adage that if you really want to learn something, you ought to teach it, this is the hidden logic of their claim: What you've figured out how to do yourself, what has become instinctual to you as a practitioner or a scholar, will remain a sort of mysterious, magical power until you ask yourself how you *actually* do it. Becoming self-aware of those practices is like being a computer that has just figured out how to explain binary to itself.

This principle suggests the paradox of our central claim that it's not about what you do but about what they do. It's *not* about what you do because teaching is about learning, mostly your students' learning. It *is* about what you do in the sense that you're teaching them some of what you know how to do, and *now you have to figure out just how the hell you do those things*, which is no small feat.

If this thought experiment is getting harder now, that's because it's as hard as the hardest and most rewarding intellectual work you've performed yourself. It's one thing to have the brilliant thought that enabled you to finish your first book, the insight that led to your first article. It's another thing to understand how you had the thought and how you can now help others think *like that*. Not to think that exact same thought but to develop the instincts and abilities that enable them to think in the special ways your discipline thinks.

Work in stages, just as you teach your students to do. First, write out what you want your students to be able to do and then name qualities you want that work to have. Think about how you do those things yourself. When you're working through a problem and trying to write about it, which activities are nonnegotiable? Which are unavoidable gateways on the path to a finished product?

Now move from you to your students. What's really going on in a student's growth over a semester of work when your assignments are calibrated well? Multiple, simultaneous forms of development that overlap, pull at one another, and feed one another. We can think of these forms of development as *narratives*, stories about how your students are being transformed by the work.

Of Students and Stories

How can we imagine the ways our students will change, the ways they might see both themselves and the material differently, as they work through a well-designed sequence of assignments?

The most concrete indicator is the growth of your students' understanding of content. That understanding is familiarly, and simply, referred to as *knowledge*—which is never one thing. We who teach will recognize the distinction between prerequisite knowledge (the knowledge brought into a class) and cumulative knowledge (the knowledge gathered, shaped, and developed over the length of the course).

Prerequisite
knowledge

Cumulative
knowledge

It's necessary to differentiate between a prerequisite *course* and prerequisite knowledge, as the former certainly doesn't guarantee the latter. As your experience has surely borne out, students routinely enter a course lacking the kinds of knowledge that your syllabus assumes they have. Some may come with more knowledge of the subject than you might at first assume, but the odds are good that most have far less. Let's leave aside the question of whether it's your responsibility to accommodate these students; you'll want some premeditated strategy in place for how you'll quickly ascertain who does and does not have this knowledge. And you'll want a plan for what to do about those who do not. These are matters of assignments, too.

This narrative is straightforward in the sense that students begin mostly lacking the knowledge they'll gain in your course. They gain it, or they don't, and then the term's over.

Of course, it's never this simple. Our first diagram of a student's movement from not-knowing to knowing isn't quite right. Students' paths to knowledge more often look like the next two drawings.

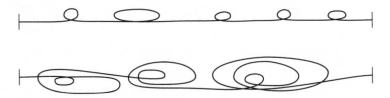

The point is that the way we gain knowledge is nonlinear and recursive, so you'll want to plot and anticipate moments of repetition, regression, leaping ahead. Student development is uneven. It's wise to remember that the apparent linearity of our syllabi can fool us into forgetting what learning is really like.

Prerequisite knowledge isn't only about facts and theories. Not just about *know*, but about *know-how*. Your students begin a semester not knowing how *to do* at least some of the things you want them to do. They lack not only prerequisite knowledge but prerequisite know-how.

This is visible when, for example, you give them a writing assignment that asks for finished work in response to what you thought was a reasonable question. You get back essays that clearly skipped steps. The evidence they mount seems picked at random. Their theses are, mostly, poorly informed opinions. "I think this or that" papers are less about thinking than opining.[1]

To opine isn't enough. (Asserting is often only opining loudly.) You're teaching thinking as process, and process stages what we write, starting here and ending there. You want your students' understanding of how to move from the beginning to the end—of any disciplinary activity—to grow over a term. At the start, they may need every step laid out for them. But by the last weeks of the semester, they may need only an end goal or just an area of focus named in the assignment.

For teachers who are experienced practitioners and thinkers in their fields, there are a number of actions that have become nearly automatic. These actions verge on or are forms

---

[1] *Opining* is a good word that gets less use and respect than it might. An *opinion* is the outcome of opining. A student might be shocked to be told that the paper is nothing more than that student's opinion, though that is probably the truth. Or shocked that you're not especially interested in an opinion and would prefer reasoned argumentation.

of embodied knowledge, something like the way a pianist's hands find solutions to potentially difficult fingerings. Experienced pianists don't need teachers to solve problems for them. Students often do. But good teachers will work to free students from their tutelage.

| Process spelled out | Fewer steps articulated | Beginning and end defined | Only end goal named |

Typically, this means crafting a syllabus that initiates a movement from a certain amount of hand-holding to an expectation that students will know how to take themselves from step to step on their own. The experience that will allow students to make such progress is partly a matter of range and repetition—trying lots of different challenges many times, failing, and then learning to succeed.

In these repetitions, students build a facility with the processes necessary to your discipline's work. They also build a set of more abstract ideas and understandings that will inform and shape their work, something like the way the keel determines a boat's handling.

In most cases, your students learn through a continual movement back and forth between concrete activities—looking at things that really happened, examining objects of analysis, following lab procedures—and abstract understandings of those activities. Students see something happening a certain way—a precipitate forming, a literary technique unmasking a character's thoughts, a price changing in a particular market—and they see several variations of these phenomena. They learn to name what is happening, to conceptualize the phenomena: solubility, interiority, elasticity.

With continued work, students survey an increasing stock of concrete material—more case studies, experiments, time spent with patients, problem sets—and thus build a larger stock of related concepts. Ideally, they become self-aware, conscious of how they are making these movements, too.

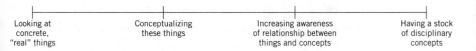

| Looking at concrete, "real" things | Conceptualizing these things | Increasing awareness of relationship between things and concepts | Having a stock of disciplinary concepts |

Facts and Concepts

If an assignment is an opportunity for you to teach your students how to think about things, then the objective of the assignment is both the thing—usually a bunch of facts, though sometimes a theory or argument or even experience—and the process of thinking about the thing (Homer's *Iliad*, thinking about Homer's *Iliad*).

The very best students will be on to this game. They'll understand that the goal of an assignment is twofold. More: They'll even develop a useful doubt about how well a concept accurately or completely maps the reality of any given phenomenon. Higher-order thinking in most disciplines involves a careful, continual evaluation of our explanatory/analytical frameworks. To get there, students need a large number of concepts in hand and opportunities to test them against various bodies of phenomena.

This movement toward greater conceptual awareness thus parallels another type of student learning: the growth of students' comfort with ambiguity and discovery of the unfinished work that drives continued research.

Facts or concepts? Facts and concepts and strategies? A good assignment may teach all of these, though we'll have a better chance of reaching our goals if we make clear to ourselves what those goals are. We often teach students simplified models—models that are perhaps even a little bit wrong—earlier in their education: the supply and demand curves of Economics 101, the equations of Newtonian physics, pH scales built entirely around H+ concentrations, or even the idea that you can't start a sentence with a conjunction. And then exceptions, caveats, or even whole competing explanatory models enter the room and give students the problem of uncertainty and the gift of nuance and paradox. They learn to think dialectically and to enter debates in your discipline, sometimes even if they're nonmajors.

| Certainty: principles, basic concepts, facts | Looking at case studies, seeing multiple approaches | Discovering debate, unfinished work of a discipline | Inquiry: competing perspectives, questions, doubt |

The development of students' comfort with ambiguity and debate is a powerful stage of cognitive maturity.[2] If the student is beginning study in a professional field, this cognitive maturity enables the student to begin to think like a practitioner. One of the open secrets of every field is the necessity of developing comfort with its most difficult or even unresolved problems. These, after all, motivate continued work in a discipline. As students learn this comfort—which is as much a kind of emotional maturity as it is intellectual development—they learn something important about the complexity of practicing your discipline and also about the complexity of the world itself. They also develop an ethics of quality—deep, moral understanding of the importance of practicing your discipline or profession the right way—and an awareness of what good work looks like. Practically, this means developing in the student an ability to evaluate one's own work and to offer quality feedback to peers. Philosophically, this means passing on the flame of our work to new generations who will understand that to practice the work well, to the highest standard, is an ethical obligation.

[2] As it surely is for us as teachers, too.

Beginning students often need some kind of rubric to make clear the standards by which their work will be judged. In such a rubric, the teacher lays out exactly what's required: the work must be so long, must adhere to such a format, must check certain boxes. But later, as the students' knowledge grows, they come to know what good work looks like from a charge they get when they see something glorious or shoddy, or from seeing a teacher react to excellent or problematic work that students, or even professionals, have done.

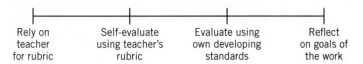

| Rely on teacher for rubric | Self-evaluate using teacher's rubric | Evaluate using own developing standards | Reflect on goals of the work |

When we talk about how to evaluate work—revealing our own perspectives and metrics—we're also preparing students to read work not their own. Grading provides a degree of the "norming" that students need, as does exposure to a wide variety of work that others have completed. "Show me your work," the teacher says to the student, but there's a different benefit in sharing what other students have done, valuable in a way that top-down, teacher-student interactions, as important as they are, cannot be.

A caveat here is that students need to learn how to articulate, in their own words, the ideas and arguments others have advanced, without flattening the complexity of those ideas. It's a key goal of teaching and learning: how to critique without judging simply—or simply judging. James Baldwin doesn't say that "racism is bad"—end of story—but students like to claim that he does.[3] To build this sense of professional ethics and

---

[3] Of course, he doesn't say it's good, either. Part of his project was to move beyond moralizing and suggest how too-simple ethical systems have enabled and even constituted racism. He *shows* how racism works and why it's so destructive to all of us. Baldwin, by the way, is an excellent resource for showing students what nuanced thought looks like and sounds like.

taste, students must first give themselves over wholly to the material before they respond to, critique, or challenge it. Like initially reluctant participants in couples therapy, they should grow into adults able to say what others have said before, and able to say it in all its richness, as though it were their own. As they mature, they gain the power and ethical ground from which to respond.

This holds true as much for their responses to, say, the political theorist Wendy Brown or to the architect Zaha Hadid as it does for their response to their peers in an in-class workshop or out-of-class peer feedback. Our planning for assignments can build in moments for careful and respectful responses.

What's most important here is for students to develop a sense of responsibility to the intellectual community in which they're participating and to which they hope one day to make a contribution. This responsibility includes a willingness to receive criticism that is made in good faith and the ability to internalize that criticism as they develop a sense of professional ethics.

Like the strongest teachers, the strongest students typically moderate a reasonable confidence with conscious self-doubt. They know they can fail, and in fact welcome productive failure from which they learn, but strive to limit failure incrementally or at least aspire to higher-order failures. And with growing to know what good work looks like comes an increasingly individualized sense of taste. Taste can mean radically different things in different disciplines and still other things depending on whether students are pursuing a course in their major or out of it. Taste is connected to specialization but also to voice and identity. What kind of practitioner, researcher, and thinker will a particular student become? How will learning to do this work in an area outside their specializations affect them in adult life?

Our students must discover this themselves through a hard-won vision of what they would like their own work—vocation or avocation—to look like, and the wisdom to know the difference between what is idiosyncratic to their aspirations and what the broader discipline requires. Knowing this difference will determine whether they can be responsible citizens of a disciplinary community. It's important that they understand community standards and avoid insisting that others adhere to rules they can rightly set only for themselves. In many courses, we don't expect that our students will ultimately practice professionally in the discipline, but we still hope that the way our discipline goes about studying the world will make up a part of how *our students* study the world in their everyday lives. Discovering who they'll be as engineers or philosophers, managers or anthropologists or graphic artists is finally the narrative of student work that matters most. And sometimes students discover part of who they'll be as engineers in a musicology course. It's the story of students becoming something more than students.

Story, however we understand it, is important. Here it's the story of how assignments become something more than assignments and how students learn to embody the practices of a discipline. It's the story of students learning how to be ambitious, how to choose the work for themselves. It's the story of students growing up. Even if a student is enrolled as a matter of meeting distribution requirements, this path toward becoming is the goal.

What do we really want? We want them to be transformed by the work they do in our courses. And we want them to want to be transformed.

In other words, the dominant narrative, the one that every other part of the developmental work you've designed aims to realize, is a story of *motivation*. We *can* teach motivation, contrary to what many of our own teachers may have believed decades ago. Motivation isn't "you've got it or you don't." As we educate more students whose parents may not have had access to higher education, let's not assume that a desire for any particular type of knowledge is some deep, intrinsic quality. A great syllabus orchestrates students' discovery of their reasons for pursuing work this term, why the course matters to them and to the world they know. It changes who they are when they're working—changes them from a captive audience doing what the teacher asks to a group of individuals excited by each new discovery. No student does excellent work—even or especially required work—they haven't *chosen* to do themselves.

Knowledge of course does not (yet) shape student's understanding of world or self

Work externalized ("The teacher is making me do this.")

Work internalized ("I am choosing to do this.")

Work fully internalized ("I do this. I am this. This matters in the world and to me.")

As we argued in our discussion of the classroom community, students need opportunities to write, think, and converse about why they're performing the work of your course. While it may sound hokey on its surface, giving students this space and taking it seriously as an intellectually rigorous part of professional practice can transform a reluctant student into an eager one.

Some idea of "knowledge" untethered from their experience of the world can feel, to students, meaningless or alienating. That's why we need to get the assignments right. The *OED* suggests the earliest, and still current, definition of *assign* as: "to allot, appoint, authoritatively determine." We could read in this definition the implication that the one doing the assigning has significant power over the one being assigned, as in one of the senses that follows under it: "to make over a convict as an unpaid servant."

Most of us hope our students don't feel as though they've been forced into indenture. But the definition also contains a competing sense—"to transfer or formally make over to another"—in which the person being assigned is given something. The assignment is not simply an "authoritative determination" that your students must do something. It is also a gift. Beyond that, the word contains a further sense of *assignment* as an appointment to "an office, duty, or fate." To be assigned is, in some ways, to *become*, to be granted a role and maybe even to be granted the fulfillment of a destiny.

Putting It All Together

As much as the diagrams above may imply complex processes of growth, students experience all these transformations through discrete assignments. Faculty ask their students to complete an enormous range of tasks: problem sets, essays, case studies, presentations, technical reports, musical performances, harmonic analyses, posters, memos, proofs, paintings. Most of the world of human activity can be assigned.

Yet we typically limit ourselves to the handful of established forms in our disciplines. In upper-level, reading-intensive courses, we ask for the response paper. In engineering, the technical report. And across many, many disciplines, at an enormous cost of class time, there's the ubiquitous presentation.

Do you actually enjoy watching student presentations? Do you get the sense that the students like doing them? What is being accomplished by the presentation (other than your nudging them not to say "like" and to stop fidgeting so much) that you can't get at any other way? When we ask students to present something, what are we testing for? Rhetorical skills, content knowledge, theatrical flair, IT facility? If we don't know—and don't make clear to the student what we expect—we've failed them before they've had the chance to exercise their agency.

Every established form of assignment has its failures that rest in plain sight, invisible because they're what we've done for so long. Many or most of these failures hinge on whether we have thought through the entire range of goals we could reach by asking students to perform this work. The care plans that nursing students write up analyze a patient's needs and build a strategy to help them, but what more could they do?

This question—what more can my students get out of *their* assignments?—starts to become more provocative when we ask it of *the totality of assignments in a syllabus* in relationship to *the story of your students' development across a term*. It can take courage to leave behind the standard assignment structures with which we're most familiar: two or three exams, or perhaps three papers, or perhaps a single big technical report, all of which function largely as an evaluative mechanism bolted onto the real course—the content the teacher delivers to students. Our syllabus might look odd to colleagues when it includes a robust body of assignments calibrated to different goals. But if student work is the engine of a course, then the assignments are the creative center of our teaching practice. That's the kind of sequence we're arguing for.

The assignments we craft are limited only by our own creativity and by our determination of their effectiveness when we try them out with real students. Assignments may enable students to become more aware of their progress in the course, or to build one particular ability that's a threshold to the bigger, more difficult work they'll do next, or to fail at a task they can't do yet—simply because you know that your students come to you not knowing how to fail, not knowing that failing well is an important skill.

Assignments might task students with going out into the world at large to find something to look at in relation to a principle, idea, or text under consideration in class. They might ask students to think through course material via a different discipline. They might ask students not to solve a technical, mathematical, or scientific problem but to explain how and why they *would* solve it a certain way.

In place of presentations, students might hold mock academic conference panels, sharing and discussing a semester's worth of work in front of an audience of students, with a goal of generating a rich intellectual conversation among the entire class. Or they might be given specific imaginary (or real) audiences to which they must calibrate a talk, paper, or poster, rather than the more immaterial and abstract idea of simply addressing the class. (When in life—including our own professional lives—do you address a group of other people without a specific purpose in mind other than to "get a good grade"?) They might invent a metaphor that translates a difficult concept into different terms, so that more people can find their way into it. Think of close reading as an act of attuning a text and reader so that they arrive at a resonant frequency— that tendency of certain objects to buzz in harmony with one another, even if they're not physically touching.

In place of a draft of a research paper, or before a draft, students might hand in a body of notes they've taken, with quotations copied out of a variety of sources together with their thinking about those quotations—a form of note-taking many of us perform in our own professional practice but that is likely to be an unfamiliar strategy to many students. That will, of course, require the teacher to explain what is at risk (taking creative or speculative chances) and what is at stake (the possibility of an intellectual payoff) in the work we all do at the beginning of a project—and how it connects to the finished work they'll eventually hand in.

Imagine assignments that are not simply about downloading a document from the course management system or opening the required textbook, assignments that force students to set foot in a library (gasp), speak with other students, or hand in notes on their own finished, already-graded work.

Take it even further: Test your students' ability to know what sort of work is necessary to achieve a goal you set by asking them to *write their own assignments*. Yes, this is not uncomplicated, but hear us out. You could grade the assignment they write, itself, for its ability to recognize what the next steps are in your course's work. Or you could grade both the assignment they've composed and the work they've done in response to it.

Should all the assignments be spelled out in the syllabus? In practice, we know that our best-laid plans *gang aft agley*. That's Scots English for getting totally screwed up. Robert Burns uses the phrase in his "To a Mouse," in which he concludes that when our plans go "agley" the result is "grief and pain" instead of something he calls "promised joy." We're not suggesting that joy is the intended outcome of giving your syllabus a rethink, but the avoidance of grief and pain does seem like a good idea.

Many of us will need to leave space for variation in the term, but all of us benefit from looking more closely at the sequence of assignments as a whole, in order to see how well it tells the stories we've laid out here. A course's assignments can be organized according to a straightforward logic of accumulation and forward movement: Assignment 1 tests the students' mastery of the material in Unit 1, Assignment 2 tests Unit 2, and so on. Or Assignment 1 makes sure students have studied the material for Class 2. But when you begin asking how Assignment 1 relates to Assignment 2 and to Assignment 3, you may find new functions for old forms, or you might discover that you want new types of assignments to accomplish your goals, which ultimately need to be, or become, the students' goals.

Now, let's deal with the other side of all this productive student work: The fact that *you* have to do something with it, as well as to make sure students show up (on time) with it, and keep them from cheating on it. Let's think about how our own work can honor and make the most of their work.

6

Our Work and How We Do It

Teach, assign, grade: three stages in what we're often imagined to do, from opening day's first chalk mark to the last keyboarded final B+. We know that grading is largely about helping students learn, but what would it look like if our grading was concerned *only* with student learning? What new opportunities can you invent to give your students meaningful feedback? What could change? What would happen if we taught students first and content second?

The syllabus conceals much. All the background preparation you've done for the upcoming semester, the books and articles read and judged, the work of selecting what readings might work, the careful development of questions and problems that don't simply create hurdles that students can clear and that you can grade, but are questions and problems the consequences of which are clear to you in advance. You've worked out a set of readings and activities that are meant to let students discover on their own many of the course's most important lessons. Yes, they'll hear them from you, but if you do it right, they'll learn from the collective experience you've been busy laying plans for.

Teachers don't want, or need, their students to know all the details that go into planning a course, though it wouldn't hurt to disabuse them of the idea that teachers go to graduate school, are assigned classes, and then show up, somehow naturally prepared to let their innate brilliance shine out spontaneously. None of us really want that to happen anyway, at least not in that way. It's useful, however, for the class to know the course you're teaching is work, for you as well as for them.

The syllabus lays out tasks, both for the class and for us teachers. The classroom is one form of a teacher's work, but for many of us it's the work just beyond the classroom that's the biggest drain on our energies: the exams, papers, and reports we have to grade. They're all there in the syllabus, their due dates marked out as defining moments in the course—and defining moments in our work flow, too.

You're in your office, or on a train, or at home, or you've been in all three of these places, dutifully lugging the stack with you but procrastinating the way academics usually procrastinate—by doing other stuff you had to do anyway.

When you look at that stack, what looks back? It's a cliché that seeing ourselves reflected in the eyes of another can reveal something meaningful about us. Your students are watching you—and so is the work they produce for you. In our assignments, we teachers see something of ourselves, our concerns, our methods. The grade we give to an assignment, and then to the student who created it, says something about us, too—about the effectiveness of our teaching, our preparation, the way we built the assignment from the raw material that the class is busy studying. There's even the double duty of the assignment you give: When you assign students work, you're also assigning yourself the task of doing something with that work. No good pedagogical deed goes unpunished.

We negotiate our way, then, through two doublings: a grade for them, a grade for us; an assignment for them, work we do once that assignment is turned in. By this point you will have memorized this book's mantra, so it's time for us to change it up slightly: It's not just about what they do or what we do. It's about *what we do with* what they do. In this chapter, let's think about the work that our students make for us—make in the sense of the work that they physically deliver and the intensive engagement on our part that it requires, and our responsibilities to the work that the syllabus marks off as stages in learning.

The Trouble with Grades

Every syllabus is supposed to say something about how the student's grade in the course will be determined. That final grade is, in turn, determined by the grades on each assignment, each quiz, each gradable measurable deliverable (as surely some administrator says with a completely straight face). Does anyone really enjoy grading? To do it well is to take on difficult, time-consuming labor, even if the only outcome is a letter grade and a few words of comment. Telling a student that she or he has done well, not so well, or even quite badly certainly introduces a cadence into a semester's music, but if that's all it accomplishes, we shouldn't be surprised if a student's response is a vigorous attempt to turn that C– into a B+ (or that C-flat into a B-sharp).

Students may know what their grades *are*, but they don't know what their grades *mean*—how rankings are arrived at, what we expect them to do next—unless we tell them. If we don't, and we choose to rely instead on the syllabus to do the whole of this work for us ("Papers 50%, Exam 30%, Class participation 20%," or some such calculation), we shouldn't be surprised by a student's confused resistance. One of the curious things about grading is that students respond viscerally to a D or an F, even if they've received that grade for an assignment weighted to make up a very small or even insignificant part of their final grade. Will you use that to your advantage, hoping it will spur them to work harder? Or do you worry that if, in week two, you're already telling them that their work is awful, you'll turn them against you? The problem of grading is that a single number or letter will, at the end of the term, stand for the collected body of a student's performance in your class, and that even individual grades, like the grade on a research project, for example, somehow must represent—and occlude—the many, many individual tasks the student had to complete to get to the final product. If you teach at an institution that provides grades (as most but not all do) you can't be entirely surprised when a student seeks more information about the grade and the process by which you arrived at it. There's inquiry, and then there's the inquiry bordering on harassment.

If you teach, you know what grade-grubbing behavior looks like—a student's tireless pursuit of an improved score for a course.[1] The "grubbing" part comes from the Old English *grubbian*, meaning "to dig," though more than one professor would suggest it comes from an early word meaning "to chip away at resistance, often by refusing to leave an office." Nobody likes a grade grubber, not even other grade grubbers.

When we perceive grade-grubbing behavior, though, we might reflect that students take tremendous risks to attend college and are desperate to see those risks culminate in the reward of a successful career. As they're young, they may not recognize the extent to which "soft skills," which employers weight more and more heavily, as well as many other factors, will determine their futures; and so they may *overvalue* the grade. But it's hard to fault them for their (often single-minded)

[1] Some colleges have killed grading entirely or have done so for first-year students. Graduate programs typically operate on a scale that's shrunk to a mere three grades (B+, A−, A), the lowest of which suggests you may not even belong in the program in the first place.

focus on your evaluation of their work. Be prepared for some conjugations of Old English *grubbian*.

It's not only our students who can feel trapped by the tyranny of grades. Many of us rebel against the reviewing and ranking culture that's emerged in our digital lives. The television series *Black Mirror* captured our growing anxiety about this tendency toward reductive scoring in everyday life. An episode entitled "Nosedive" concerns Lacie Pound, a young woman who exists in a world where anyone we meet can score us, at every encounter (partygoer, coworker, gas station attendant), resulting in a simple, aggregate number between one and five. This score determines the social and economic opportunities to which people have access, so it's a dead-serious business. But because of the ease with which anyone can hurt or help your score, everyday social and work interactions become increasingly superficial, everyone pandering to get a five-star rating.

While faculty strive to evaluate student work in much deeper ways than we see in *Black Mirror*'s dystopian vision, many of us still try to sidestep the superficiality of the letter or number grade by offering additional feedback along with the score. We comment in the margins and at the end of papers, meet with students one-on-one, and find ways to provide feedback in class.

But there's still, at the end of the day, the score. And much like the crisis in "Nosedive," your score of the student's work, when aggregated with the scores other faculty provide, may indeed have a powerful effect on the opportunities that a student will have, at least in the immediate years beyond your classroom. Evaluation is a serious business, in some ways the *most* serious business we conduct.

Grading begets other difficulties, too. Many, many faculty have had the uncomfortable experience of being contacted by a dean or other administrator after having given a student a bad grade: Would it be possible for us to raise it, either so the student can pass the course or so the student (or a parent) will leave the dean alone? Tenured faculty can try to resist these requests. Adjunct faculty may have no choice but to leave standards behind and make the problem go away.

Then there's the enigma—or specter—of grade inflation, which can be a problem, perhaps especially at prestigious universities, where students who are used to continual, unending praise and success expect no different in their college careers. The cynical slogan "Gold in, gold out" is invoked by critics of elite colleges, which, enjoying the cream of the high school crop, have little more to do with their glistening recruits than to polish them brightly. We agree that this characterization is unfair to hardworking students at elite schools, but it's sustained by the perception that top institutions avoid sullying the brand with poor grades.

Grade inflation seems to bear some correlation to the rising cost of college. As one student we overheard said, "Who's going to pay $50,000 for a 2.7?" This is the economic logic of grading in a different sense, a trend that's seen increasingly as another consequence of the "neoliberal" university, where our students are now spoken of, with insufficient irony, as "customers." As department store magnate Harry Gordon Selfridge put it at the beginning of the twentieth century, *the customer is always right*, which, whether true or not, has become a law of commercial transactions. Mega-stores and universities have become aggregates of departments. Sociology and luggage on floor two or, increasingly, page two of a website.

Bad grades aren't just an economic problem for colleges that need to keep paying customers enrolled. They're an economic problem for faculty, who face tremendous pressure to conduct research and publish in their fields. Giving bad grades means students will ask more of our time, show up for office hours, and write us emails ("Hey professor" or simply "Hey") asking for help.

To be clear, if we're doing our jobs, giving bad grades forces us to *teach harder* and to figure out how we could—ethically, honestly—*give better grades*. Because getting students to excel, and to fully earn the best possible grades in the study of challenging subjects, is a goal for any teacher obligated to provide quantitative rankings of student work, either by numerical or alphabetical designations. No teacher wants students to fail, but to sort the reasons for student failure is a time-consuming undertaking.

The laws of clock and calendar apply to us teachers as well as to our students. We all work with limited time; teachers have to calculate how much time they can spare for teaching, especially junior faculty members facing down a tenure review or adjuncts who have to scramble among gigs at three different colleges, as well as any of us who try, however simply, to maintain some semblance of a family or social life. But if we're going to be tough and honest, with both our class and ourselves, we also have to carve out enough time to help students learn from the difficult experience of failure. Failure can sometimes teach what no other prepared lesson can manage and do it more quickly and more memorably. Failure—by which we mean failure that's fully understood—is a tough learning tool, but a learning tool all the same.

We should mention that adding to the complexity of grading is the problem of evaluative bias. In certain disciplines, right and wrong are clearly defined: The answer isn't 11.62, and there's no conceivable way it *could be* 11.62. But much of the time, there is ambiguity not only in *how* right a student's work is but in how we set up that work in the first place. The SAT and many other forms of standardized testing have come under fire for judging students' backgrounds as much as their ability.[2] Certain questions hinge on the cultural/literary/social contexts with which students are comfortable rather than on their intellectual ability. Certain types of prompts set students from one background more at ease than students from another. We can make assumptions, looking out into a classroom and seeing the actively engaged student and assuming she or he will produce good work, while the quiet, recessive student at the next desk seems a candidate for less impressive results. Good teaching requires that we set aside first impressions, and even second ones. Our syllabus lays out goals and principles, including the invocation of academic integrity, to be followed by students and by ourselves. Once laid out, those principles are ours to protect and sustain. We must work to be as fair in our assessments as we expect students to be in applying themselves to the tasks assigned and to the completion of assignments.

How then, other than by means of grades, can we provide students with an incentive to work? As we've argued over the course of this book, it would be disastrous if a grade were the *only* or even the most important spur to learning. We want to believe that that's what motivation, desire, and curiosity are for. But we know from experience that many of our students come to us valuing grades above all else, so we may as well make the most of the carrot and stick that rest on the shelf, awaiting our grasp.

The task, then, is to use grades to transform student motivation from something simple and owned by us into something deep and owned by them, to invent motivation that lives beyond and above the B sitting mutely on a transcript. Let's

---

[2]One flashpoint among many was María Veronica Santelices and Mark Wilson's "Unfair Treatment? The Case of Freedle, the SAT, and the Standardization Approach to Differential Item Functioning," *Harvard Educational Review* 80, no. 1 (April 2010): 106–34.

leave behind *correcting* as a verb to describe what we do with student work. Let's instead try to find things we can do that are directly connected to verbs *students will own*. To do that, though, we first have to reboot the students' idea of grading.

What will work best for you? With your students? In distributing syllabi on the first day of class, some teachers already begin the work of revising their students' understanding of grades. "Yes, you see a grade breakdown here, and yes, those grades do, in fact, measure your performance in my class, but you should know that they're actually made up of many, many smaller opportunities for you to do great work, and that I see my role in that work as collaborative and supportive. You will ultimately get the grade you deserve, and I don't guarantee you won't fare badly, even if you try hard. But I want very much for you to earn a good grade, and I'll do everything I can to help you get there."

For such a strategy to work, it's crucial to think about grading within coursetime. In students' minds, the most important grade we give is the last, final grade. But from a teaching perspective, the first grade is usually the most important.

Here's why. The first grade sets the standard by which individual students will start judging their own work. It's an act of calibration, attuning students' expectations for the type and quality of work you want and for the exertion required to make it. And usually, first grades are low.

But why are they low? The explanation for this is simple, or at least it's simple to the experienced teacher. *Most of your students are taking your class because they don't already know how to do the thing you're teaching them to do.* It's not—we emphasize—about the content they don't already know but about the way of working with and thinking about that content, a mode of productive reflection that they don't already know how to make a part of their lives. Many students have never thought about grades, or school, this way before. Even if the way we grade a first assignment is calibrated to students' beginning ability level, so that what earns an A early in the term is different from what will earn an A later in the term, students need to understand what the goal is and that there will be challenges in getting there.

It takes courage to hand back a stack of first exams or essays or problem sets with a lot of bad grades on them. It takes courage for a teacher to be honest, but let's not forget that it takes courage on the students' part to hand in that first piece of work, too. If we can communicate to them that the uninflated, honest grade we've given them is an act of genuine care—not simply by saying it, though that doesn't hurt—they will have reason to believe that thoughtful feedback is *careful* feedback, careful because both rigorous and sensitive, thoughtful because about real work by real students.

Feedback, Feed Forward

Let's pause for a moment to consider a bit further what we mean when we refer to *feedback*. *Merriam-Webster* gives, as its initial meaning, "the return to the input of a part of the output of a machine, system, or process." In the ensuing century, the word's use has been extended to all manner of metaphorical senses, yet *feedback*'s mechanistic overtones persist. It's dangerously easy to evaluate one's own feedback system by mechanical or cybernetic standards. Some classrooms aspire to that—the on/off binary of correct/incorrect, whether or not the material lends itself to that sort of reductive clarity. Even when we're not tempted by binary options, most of us tend to be less creative than we could be in thinking about what kinds of responses we might give students and what those responses might *do* for them.

What if we thought of what we do with student work not as "providing feedback" but simply as teaching, or better, helping students learn? For lack of a better single word, we'll continue to use *feedback* in this chapter, but we hope you'll modify your sense of it to focus on student learning. Let's try to hear nourishment in the word *feedback*—the "feed" of nurture, not the "feed" of digital delivery.

One way to communicate this is to treat your students' first few grades as provisional. In many classes, that first D isn't set in stone, and it won't necessarily affect students' final grades, so long as they can figure out what the D *means* and learn from it how to do better work. Maybe they can do the assignment again and have the new grade either replace the original or get averaged with it. Another technique some teachers use is to give the first "real" grade only after several prior opportunities for lower-stakes feedback: ungraded work, oral or written feedback, work scored pass/fail or with a check, check-minus, or check-plus. Still other teachers turn back graded work to be further revised but turned in only when accompanied by a cover sheet in which the student analyzes what the revision has done. Some teachers choose to meet one-on-one with students in the wake of the first grade, a critical moment when the opportunity to sit down and speak directly can change students' understanding of their work. In such meetings, the teacher can make clear that the grade evaluates the success of this one, particular piece of work, *not* the students themselves, their potential, their effort, or their personalities. Our students make their work, but they *aren't* their work. It's a message good teachers have to communicate again and again.

One might also imagine a brief writing assignment, whether out of class or in class, called something like "My Best C." "Describe a moment when you received a bad grade," we might say to students, "and how that grade ultimately helped you." If students have never received such a grade—grade inflation isn't just a college problem—we might ask them to look at other areas of their lives where they've received the equivalent of a bad grade: a parent disappointed at a poor choice they've made, a friendship lost, a mistake that cost them something dear.

All these approaches to changing student perception of grades, whichever strategy you pursue, need to be at least somewhat premeditated and will be most effective if they're directly noted in the syllabus. That might mean expanding your syllabus to include an additional paragraph about how grades work in your course. It's tricky, especially in the hands of the student whose close reading skills are most evident in a search for what the syllabus allows. Doing so, however, can begin that difficult work of reducing grubbing and helping students build an ethics of quality.

One overriding rule regardless of your methods of teaching and evaluation: Students must believe that teachers are providing fair evaluations of their work and, crucially, must understand *why* they did poorly, not in terms of effort but in terms of the distance between excellent work and what they handed in. What specific problems resulted in the lower grade, and what steps can students take to improve?

What gets marked on a student's paper? Writing or typing out comments is different from *correcting* student work, even if we often speak of those very different activities as if they were the same. Extensively line-editing a paper or report, or scribbling in correct equations or stages in a series of calculations, might make us feel as though we're working hard. And we are. Yet our effort—grueling or not—has little to do with the *student's* effort. We're trained in how to do the work of our discipline. And until we train them, our students—with their green thoughts, in papers that are sometimes composed of redundant and obvious observations arranged in ungrammatical sentences—are not. Of course, not all papers are like that, but our responsibility to the train-wreck paper is perhaps greater than it is to the beautifully executed paper—or at least it's not a jot less.

But if we're handing back papers covered with corrections we've made to the students' grammar and style, we are robbing them of the opportunity to do that work themselves. Worse, we are signaling to students that their problems are primarily grammatical or mechanical, when most line-level writing problems stem from underdeveloped thinking.

Students—like the rest of us—write poorly when they don't know entirely what it is they want to say or why they're saying it. They won't care about grammar or come to need more sophisticated sentence structures until they feel an urgent need to express complex ideas.[3] Similarly, students screw up calculations when they haven't understood the principles underlying the math. They won't do the work well until they understand why they're doing it and how it fits within their developing mental map of your subject.

Line-editing student work is the gift that keeps on disappearing—if you are the one doing it. If a student learns best by doing, then the work of line-editing—an easy but laborious thing for you; laborious and not so easy for your student—provides technical knowledge that just might survive beyond the current semester.

So we encourage you to resist the temptation to correct more than a sampling of a paper's errors. Turning work back for a fully corrected redraft may be a small piece of a larger revision strategy. It's not hard to extend this principle to other

---

[3] Probably all of us have made the mistake of thinking that we can offer a lesson on periodic sentences or "not only ... but also." Getting them to the ideas that would require those structures is another matter.

tasks that, like reading and writing, make up the core of our scholarly and professional work.

At the end of the term, when there are no more assignments to complete, no more classes to teach, our primary job is to reach a cumulative assessment. Up until that point, the feedback we offer students always *anticipates what they will do next*. A weak paper or poor performance on an exam becomes an opportunity for us to discern not just *that* students aren't doing the work well but also *why* they're coming up short.

We have to give bad grades, at least sometimes. If that's going to happen, we have to let the bad grades do their work. But how? One teacher we know first hands back papers with only a few line-level and marginal comments, asking students to reread their own work and consider its quality according to a rubric laid out in class that day. Only later do students receive their grade, with the final comments, in an email, along with an admonishment that the teacher is happy to discuss the grades with students *but only after several days have passed*. After the bad grade has sunk in—and the urge to fight back has faded—a meaningful conversation about how to improve is far more likely than in the heat of a student's disappointment. Other teachers might collect work that students *think* is finished and hand it back with the grade the teacher *would have* assigned, now with the requirement that students do one more iteration of the work.

Still another approach is to ask students to grade their own work. This practice may sound radical or foolish—there's no way they know enough to evaluate the work, that's why you're the teacher—but if we pause to consider how students earn *good grades*, the rationale for letting them grade their work becomes more clear.

Why, and how, do successful students succeed? In most cases, A students make A work because they know what A work looks like and have learned how to make it. How else would they do it? C students make C work because they *don't* know what A work looks like and *haven't* learned how to make it. Of course, the solution to this problem isn't as simple as showing C students A work and letting them figure out the rest, because learning to make A work means learning both how to recognize the A-ness of A work and how to perform the constituent tasks that culminate in A work.

So students will need to see examples of lots of (different) ways of doing those constituent tasks and be given opportunities to practice those tasks. And they must develop the ability to discern when they're doing them better or not as well. Don't underestimate the consequence of a negative critique: The first bad grade students receive is made more powerful because it belongs to the students, so long as we've convinced them that it is, indeed, theirs. Ownership begins when students realize that they have to do something next, something that hinges on what they didn't manage to do before.

We want our students to care about the material and about the work they're assigned to do. What else in life works like the "submit and forget" approach that marks so much schoolwork? As professionals and scholars, we know that the process we go through when we prepare research for publication or for a conference—drafting and redrafting—is a sort of grading we enact upon ourselves. We make a version, decide it deserves a C, and then rework it until it's up to our standards.

In order to grow in their abilities, students need to begin seeing their work in a similar way. So they need opportunities to begin—just begin—learning how to see it as an expert does. When asking students to grade their own work, we find a surprising range of ways in which they get it right and wrong. Either because they're trying to please the teacher—to show they're willing to learn—or because they genuinely get that their work is not up to snuff, many students will aim low, hitting themselves with Cs and Ds. When you see this pattern, it suggests that students have begun to accept that you'll have high standards and that you value honesty. That's useful on its own. In fact, very rarely, in conducting such experiments in grading, do teachers see students overvalue their work en masse. The C student giving himself an A is the exception rather than the rule. How your students respond to this kind of exercise will tell you something about what they've learned so far—about grading, about the work, about themselves.

Performing such an exercise, students will have to think carefully about the standards by which they're judging the work. Do they even know enough to evaluate it? What *don't they know* that they need to know to evaluate it? A student deciding that she can't grade the thing because she doesn't know how to do it right is a fine outcome, too. Offering students an opportunity to evaluate their own work before they find out how you've evaluated it puts them in an active role. Now they're not simply waiting for you to tell them how they did: They're trying to develop the ability to see what's right, what's less right or less wrong, what needs to be better, and how to get there.

If you're still with us, you know that we think every aspect of a syllabus is interconnected, within itself and with the everyday life of the classroom. Which means that assignments and feedback should be considered together. The time-intensive, largely thankless, nearly invisible work of providing feedback is about the specifics of work produced by individual students as well as the broader lessons about the classroom community, insights that only the teacher is in a position to reach because only the teacher carries the burden of responding to every piece of work by every student. We began this chapter with a discussion of grading, why it's more complicated than your students know, and why it's most meaningful when its judgmental function is teamed with its coaching function.

Whatever else you say on your syllabus about grades—
"Grades on the exams will count for 60% of your final letter
grade," "Grades on all papers will be given equal weight," and
so on—a grade is less and more than it appears. It's less when
there's no follow-up, when the grade a student receives on an
assignment is the end of the conversation about the assignment. That's when the grade is working like sugar—a quick
metabolic sprint before the inevitable valley. When a piece of
graded work is connected to a process—a self-edit and the exchange of papers, a review of notes leading up to the next iteration, a rewrite, or drafts for a mathematical proof—then
the work of grading has a chance of operating less like sugar
and more like protein, turning more slowly into energy and
lasting longer.

But what will *you* do to make this possible? What do
you expect you'll need to focus on in your feedback on the
first, second, third assignment? In what ways will the second assignment offer students an opportunity to improve
on what they did poorly in the first, and how will it add
new work, at which many students will, inevitably, fail on
their first try?

Much of this book has been discussing the many activities
we can ask students to perform. Here, let's consider the many
activities we can ask ourselves to perform. Which brings us
back to that potentially nourishing term *feedback*. The feeding comes in many forms. There's written feedback, numerical feedback, oral feedback. Some professors have tried recording audio or video feedback, marking work up digitally
via Google Docs, the "track changes" feature in Word, or using
a tablet and stylus. Sometimes simply using a form of feedback with which students are unfamiliar can help them pay
more attention to it—help them, that is, to find the feeding
that's being offered and regard it as sustenance rather than
with suspicion.

We're all familiar with the pattern of students receiving the feedback we carefully wrote up and focusing only on the grade. Who hasn't had the experience of spending hours and hours marking up student work, only to discover later that they never really did anything with it? How many teachers end the term with a pile of uncollected final papers, each heavy with commentary that will never be read?[4]

So we find ourselves among the fun-house mirrors of teaching and learning again. If your feedback will lead students toward some kind of rewrite or second attempt at the work, you have an opportunity to craft new assignments that are specific to individual students. If, as we hope it does, your syllabus has planned out a sequence of activities that are progressive and add new skills and challenges as the term goes on, feedback always opens the way to the next new assignment.

But let's be reasonable. Of course we all have time constraints. In a large lecture course, the instructor isn't going to be able to use grading to design work for individual students. Even in smaller classes, our time is limited, and there is an increasing concern that the types of intensive teaching toward which we're being urged (and to which this book admittedly sometimes urges you) can lead to burnout.[5]

So while we're suspicious in general of applying the standard of efficiency to teaching and learning, let's admit here

[4]This dilemma is, of course, structural. Work due at the last class often never sees its author again. A syllabus that moves forward the delivery of final work by a week or more gives the teacher a chance to turn the last class meeting into a teaching session about that final work, but to do that effectively means compressing the time allotted in the syllabus to earlier assignments. It's the question of coursetime again.

[5]See, for example, Jane S. Halonen and Dana S. Dunn, "Does 'High-Impact' Teaching Cause High-Impact Fatigue?," *Chronicle of Higher Education*, November 27, 2018. Note the language here: *High-impact* is the language of the business world, though it's certainly getting harder to tell business-ese apart from college-administrative-ese.

that we often have to get the most we can from limited teaching time. What patterns do you notice across the students' work, and how can you design new work for the entire class that addresses those patterns? Teachers working in disciplines where students will be tested via exams can design methods of evaluation that make it easier to discern these patterns, using a (dreaded or beloved) rubric or building a mechanism into scoring multiple-choice tests that makes easily visible where students are falling short. Whatever you do, the point is to find methods that work for you and for your students, to signal these methods and their ethos in your syllabus, and to stick as well as you can to your plan.

Honesty and Other Best Policies

Thou shalt not cheat. The modern syllabus burdens today's teachers with all sorts of responsibilities, including the responsibility to explain—and enforce—the institution's academic honesty policy, a policy that effectively becomes a part of our grading policy. Most academic honesty policies are quite similar, different primarily in length and level of detail though not in principle.

Why do students cheat? Why do they plagiarize? Do they know, not know, convince themselves otherwise?

Cheating has some causes we can't do much about. Maybe our students are working too many hours outside of school, trying to make ends meet. They're facing a stressful family situation or an exciting new relationship or the demise of one. Their days are compressed by a long commute to school. They're trying to get out from under crushing depression.

Then there is another set of seemingly simpler reasons for cheating. They ran out of time. They were incredibly anxious to get a good grade. They didn't understand some crucial aspect of the work and felt they couldn't figure it out before the work was due.

What's our part in those causes of cheating? And do the rote academic honesty policies we're obligated to include in our syllabi do anything to address them? Probably not much, other than to cover us (and the institution) legally when we catch someone.

We spell out what constitutes plagiarism in a static document students tend not to read. Or, more accurately, our departments or colleges spell it out, because we're not the ones who wrote those policies, which usually have little or nothing to do with *preventing* dishonesty and everything to do with punishing it.

Some of us have developed approaches to the academic honesty policy that work better. Perhaps we preface our university's boilerplate policy with our own address directly to our own students. We might say something about the nature of learning, that it requires making mistakes, and that it is therefore actually in a student's best interest to hand in something imperfect (rather than something that attempts to pretend perfection). We might say something about the disrespect that cheating shows toward one's peers, leaving ourselves out of it for now. We might also say something about our trust in students, that the teacher-student relationship is special and carries with it obligations on both our parts. Because it is, and does.

Academic honesty *sounds* cut and dried, a yardstick that remains eminently clear and available for measuring out campus justice without much further interrogation. But real life scenarios make the application of academic honesty regulations more complicated than that. Art professors know very well that we can quickly become embroiled in much headier stuff than boilerplate policies usually admit. If your assignment isn't a written paper, what might be considered as stealing someone's work? When are you imitating and thus commenting on someone's work? When are you influenced or inspired by someone's work? Sometimes, in fact quite often, teachers must ask students to do work that isn't "original," and this short-circuits many of the approaches we have for avoiding cheating. It's not a student's job to invent a fourth law of thermodynamics, at least not in an introductory course. We don't want originality that distracts from necessary facts; India became a republic in 1950, and that date is nonnegotiable. Further, many teachers feel that our educational system overvalues a particular form of originality. They're not looking for an original solution to a problem that has only one solution; an original solution means the student has likely found the wrong answer. How can we ensure that students are doing their own work in these cases?

Given all these challenges, we may want to accept that the academic honesty policy is *not* the best weapon—much less a simple one—for fighting cheating. If you've done your syllabus right, though, other parts of it can help. As we've suggested elsewhere, assignments are where the rubber meets the road for student learning, and the same holds true for academic honesty. Being creative in our prompts can avert some of the major sources of cheating. This means writing assignments that enable students to focus on the *how* of the work—showing steps, for example, or turning in drafts, no matter how messy, no matter how many splotches of coffee or Diet Coke. Math profs almost always want to see *how* students got to a solution. The moral here is simple: If we design a syllabus to teach process, then assignments that clearly value process change the terms within which students do their work. Even a relatively rote exercise can become both engaging and hard to fake.

Many teachers whose coursework consists largely of papers have learned to avoid widely assigned prompts—write five pages on fate in *Antigone*; explain John Stuart Mill's conception of liberty in three. One of their simplest tactics is the comparison assignment (How does John Stuart Mill's conception of liberty help us understand Antigone's decision?) or a similar juxtaposition of materials. It's not just about outfoxing the internet's system of temptations. It's a means of creating new angles of thought from which your students can explore ideas.

Cheating is fleeing. A student who engages in academic dishonesty has momentarily withdrawn from the classroom community. Even if you don't expose the student's violation in front of the class (you won't, of course), students know when something has gone wrong and one of their own has stumbled hard.

There are other ways to stumble hard, of course, like not showing up.

Anyone who's worked a bad office job knows what it's like when we are required to appear but not necessarily to be *all there*. Waiting tables, fixing someone's plumbing, nursing, these are jobs where, if we're not doing the work, it's obvious that we're not doing the work. But in a bad office job, your job is to *look* busy.

Classroom attendance can too often resemble the bad office job, requiring that students' bodies show up, even if their minds are elsewhere. Clock in, clock out. You may put in your hours, but those hours mostly get spent surfing the Web, checking and rechecking social media accounts, making small talk. That description of a workday could too easily describe many students' approaches to class time: They're following the letter of the law—in at 9:00, out at 9:50—but flouting, or flogging, its spirit and yours. Online teaching can make these difficulties even worse. Is your student paying attention or ordering a new pair of sneakers? (Are you?)

Such problems start from a misrecognition by the students and sometimes by the teacher: The classroom appears to be a cubicle, where one sits and stares at a screen, when in fact it's much closer to the basement of a house, where one struggles to get the sewer line unclogged and the hot and cold water going to the right places. A student who is physically present can be pedagogically absent.

Of course, students can also be physically *and* pedagogically absent (if they're the former, they're usually the latter, too). Just like you, we've worried that students will strive to *use up* their available absences—if the syllabus says they can miss two classes before their grades are affected, they'll go ahead and miss two classes. You can count on that. And then there are those students who miss much, much more class. When we've had a semester where one or more students have missed significant class time, we revisit our attendance policy, looking for something it might do to guard against *that* happening again.

Your syllabus tries to keep your students present, both physically and pedagogically. Perhaps it directly addresses what it really means to *attend*, right there in the attendance policy:

> You must be in class every day, full stop. Taking this course is a choice, one that you have made. I'm glad you made it, and I'm excited to work with you, together, in class. Please show respect to your classmates, to yourself, and to me by arriving on time for every class period, ready to work. If an emergency—death in the family, your own significant illness—will prevent you from attending, you *must* check in with me in advance of class via email. Please use the subject line "Unable to attend class." Remember that our classroom is a community, one that functions only if we all contribute to it. Students who do not attend class weaken our community. They also risk failure.

Your department may require a more explicit, numerical calculation of consequences, which is fine, too. But it's the spirit, the intentionality, that we care about most here.

Still, we'll always deal with chronically late or absent students. There are those moments where we wallow in the futility of noting, out loud, the attendance of a classroom that's only 75 percent full; the students who are the problem aren't there to hear our disappointment. And there's the rub, for you can't say much to a student who's not there. As with many other parts of a plan for the semester, the earliest part of the term is important for setting expectations. Make a point of speaking with students who have been absent or late as soon as the problem materializes, and you may nip it in the bud, especially if the conversation—it's got to be a conversation—works from questions for the student:

> YOU: What happened the other day?
> STUDENT: What do you mean?
> YOU: You weren't in class, why?
> STUDENT: Uhhhhh . . . My boss changed my shift at the last minute.
> YOU: That's rough, and unfair, but you know you *need* to be in class to do the work.
> STUDENT: It won't happen again.

And while there's no guarantee that it won't, you've just made clear that you noticed the student was gone, that you're paying attention to each individual in (or out of) the room.

Sometimes, and more and more often, students disappear due to significant mental health challenges. We're not psychologists (you may be one), but it's clear that anxiety and depression are troubling many, many young people—and plenty of us teachers, too. This is a particularly difficult reality of the classroom to which we can't offer any easy solutions, because there aren't any. Showing care, making accommodations, treating students as the real, complex humans they are—these help, but they get you only so far. Build relationships with counselors and administrators in student affairs or your college's wellness center so they can do their jobs.

As teachers we all try hard to help, and we believe that the work we're asking students to do *could help*. And we do our best not to mistake the academic damage wrought by crushing depression for simple laziness. If these students had the confidence to say so, they would tell us, as in a difficult relationship, "It's not you, it's me." And they'd probably really mean it.

So we focus on what we and what they *can* do. It's your students' job to attend, and part of our job is to help them want to attend. Let's turn to what we do in class and how it can help them truly *attend*.

Our job has many obligations. Get them to show up, keep them flying straight, evaluate, give feedback, reevaluate, give more feedback, and then get them to keep showing up, continue to fly straight. All this is in addition to—but not really any more important than—the content that, at least in theory, you've been engaged to teach.

What we teachers do is always going to be largely invisible work—and that's a good thing. To reveal to your students everything you've done to make the class possible, including your attentive assessment of the range of student needs and degrees of achievement, would be to tilt the playing table, letting your labor itself be a subject for your student's direct attention. It shouldn't be. Too much conscious display of what we do as teachers runs the risk of moving the focus away from what your students are doing and of setting you even further from them. You're already the teacher. To make a learning community, keep the spotlight on what students do—the work they make, the steps they take to make it better—even if those steps are all a function of your own hard-won thinking.

7

What Does Learning Sound Like?

How do you judge whether the time you and your
students spend together in class—or, for that matter,
in office hours—is really helping them learn?

Your classroom is primed for discussion. Students have done
the reading you planned out in the syllabus. They've completed the assignment, which was connected to the reading.
They've read—actually read—your feedback on their most recent work, because you made a plan that got them to read it.
They've arrived with ideas, opinions, and even a little excitement. You've primed them even more by asking them to do
some writing at the start of class, so they aren't starting cold.

This is one of the things your syllabus was working toward,
this moment, right here, right now. You think of it as an
important day because the material is critical to the story your
course tells.

Discussion begins. What do you hear, and how do you hear
it? You know that your focus should be on what the students
are saying far more than on what you are saying. In fact, you've
learned to try to get out of the way as much as possible. Several students become more animated as they connect the reading to current events. Another chimes in with an anecdote
that connects to those same events. Another follows with an
anecdote connected to the anecdote.

Are they going off the rails, already? Do you need to intercede, reorient them? If you do, will your directiveness mean that you're falling back into a mode of top-down teaching you've been trying to avoid? But if you don't, will the lesson fall apart?

Even in a discussion that stays on target, that hews closely to your design, you might arrive at the end of a period and wonder what, exactly, you and your students have to show for all this talk. We've all experienced this feeling, walked the line between too much control and not enough. We've all suspected that discussion can—too often—amount to mere idle chatter, that *class time itself* too often comes to an end without a clear sense of what was accomplished.

The last chapter reflected on the complexities of evaluating student work. It asked how our syllabus can lay out plans for grading and feedback that might improve the odds our students get something out of all this—the work we set up for them to do, the work they do, the work we do on the work they do.

But the last chapter also avoided the question of the participation grade, and you may not have noticed. Why? We typically don't pay much attention to it.

Some teachers have complex rubrics for grading participation, keeping a tally of student contributions each day, which they'll ultimately use in a mathematical calculation at end of term in the noble pursuit of fairness. But for most of us, such approaches are an odd fit. If we're honest with ourselves, we tend to use participation to justify bumping students' final grades up or down, according to our sense of an individual student's effort. It feels strange to grade someone's momentary contributions to a discussion, too close to that social media scoring dystopia we evoked earlier. In truth, the thing we call participation isn't a question of grading. It's a question of learning, more or less exclusively, and most of us are better off setting it apart from grading so that we can see it for what it is: a chance to communicate directly with our students, to build the classroom community we want, and to get the most out of the few hours we get to *study together*. Because that is what class time is for: to study together.

So, what does it mean to study together? How do we offer feedback in the moment, in those nicks of time our syllabus tried to anticipate and enable? And how, in the heat of these moments, can we evaluate whether our teaching is working?

If you want to see what's really happening with your students, the classroom is just as important a place as their essays or exams. Your syllabus works toward two things: The student alone, as an individual, finding new ideas, abilities, perspectives. And the students together, building knowledge, which means building the social, learning how to know, *with one another*.

You can only just glimpse the first—the student alone—and many students will lock their experience of learning away from you entirely, even if it *is* happening, even sometimes especially *because it's happening*. The considered life is a lonely thing, always, for us all, for no one else will ever inhabit the bone-box of your head. "You don't know what's in my head!" declares a small child, proudly, defiantly. Some years later, the child's father is at work on the book you're reading. This is a problem as old as knowledge itself, and the child's defiant pride becomes a lesson as old as learning itself.

But there's that other thing that the syllabus works toward, a quality or condition we might call *the knowing among one another*. And you can see as much of that kind of knowing as you want to see, at least within the confines of your three hours a week with your students. Here, in a school, we can try to learn *with one another* in the spirit of honesty rather than interest, of truth rather than getting ahead or keeping up. The considered life is a crowded thing, always, for us all, for it demands our empathetic engagement with others, other ideas, other ways of knowing. *This is the core of learning, and it is knowledge itself.*

Here's what we know about the syllabus: It's a pedagogical contract that invents a community through knowledge—a community alive in textbooks and essays, films and musical scores, methods and classifications. And we invent it through work, through exams and papers, presentations and discussions, notes, and feedback.

Here's what we know about the classroom: It happens in a space, whether physical or virtual. There's no such thing as an empty classroom. Either it's a roomful of people learning, or it's just a room.

Group Improvisation

At several points in this book we've made noises about noises. In the classroom, we see our students, and that's important. But what's more important is that, in the classroom, we *hear* them.

A classroom can be a cacophonous space, one that feels much more like the wild, even random complexity of experimental music than like the orderly, structured sonority of Mozart or Haydn. Sometimes it's hard to hear what's happening because it's fast, too fast, so that the teacher can barely keep up with the students' conversation. Sometimes it's hard to hear because it's so slow: You're getting so little from students that you feel trapped, having either to do too much yourself or to suffer through the silence of students who seem checked out.

We might have an idealized sense of what we want our classroom to sound like, one cultivated by movies (the inspiring professor! the passionate, revolutionary student!) or by our own experiences of college. But when it comes down to it, are we sure we know what we're listening for? Does good pedagogy have a distinct acoustic?

In thinking this through, it might be easier to start from a smaller classroom, the smallest one imaginable: one teacher, one student. The hydrogen atom of pedagogy. Subtract either the teacher or the student, and it's no longer a classroom. At this scale, there's less to get in the way of our work discerning what we're listening for and then hearing it. In a thoughtful essay that might change how you think about your college's writing center, Stephen M. North offers an insight that helps us understand these noisy, busy moments of classroom work to which our syllabus has carried us. He argues that tutors should evaluate their success

> in terms of changes in the writer. Rather than being fearful of disturbing the "ritual" of composing, they observe it and are charged to change it: to interfere, to get in the way, to partici-pate in ways that will leave the "ritual" itself forever altered.[1]

If we extend North's conception of teaching from one-on-one to one-with-many, our job is to intercede meaningfully in stu-dent learning, to show them new ways to learn and new ways to practice learning and the knowledge-making of our respec-tive disciplines. We get in the way of knowledge practices that may be leading them the wrong way or no way at all.

Let's think of learning as something we practice, like a dance sequence, a golf swing, a set of scales. We practice so many things, so many small and intricate skills and rituals, though the most important ones in our lives often fall outside the idea of practice: how to love, how to respect oneself and others, how to learn. We talk about lessons from life: "I learned my lesson," you say, when some act of poor judgment back-fires, or we "put into practice" something we've learned in theory, which merely means we are applying what we've

---

[1] Stephen M. North, "The Idea of a Writing Center," *College English* 46, no. 5 (September 1984), 439.

learned. Yet neither of these common expressions gets to the complex heart of learning, at least not what we mean by classroom learning. Lessons from life, we hear often, are worth more than lessons in the classroom, which assumes that the experience of organized study is somehow less valid than the world of work, whether paid or unpaid. And of course, the work of the classroom is all the more precious because it may be the most intensive and—for some students, the only—time in their lives when learning itself is the subject, when practicing how to learn is a communal undertaking.

Because *that*—more than any subject or theory or formula— is what we teach. A certain Professor Obama's syllabus for a course titled "Current Issues in Racism and the Law" at the University of Chicago was constructed almost entirely around discussions led by the professor and then, later in the term, by small groups of students.[2] Professor Obama charges his students with putting together reading packets (up to fifty pages). He then has the students place several copies of these packets on reserve in the library in advance of their group presentations. The presentations that follow "can be in the form of a debate, a free-form discussion [among presenters], a theatrical presentation, whatever." The presentations are meant to spur a meaningful conversation among all members of the class. Lest that word *whatever* signal a lack of seriousness, Professor Obama delineates clear expectations for these presentations. They must "draw out the full spectrum of views on the issue you're dealing with," show "rigor and specificity" in discussing these competing views, and weave the specific topic under discussion into the broader narrative of the course. In

[2] Barack Obama, "Current Issues in Racism and the Law," syllabus, Spring 1994, http://www.nytimes.com/packages/pdf/politics/2008OBAMA_LAW/Obama _CoursePk.pdf, provided in Jodi Kantor, "Inside Professor Obama's Classroom," *The Caucus* (blog), July 30, 2008, https://thecaucus.blogs.nytimes.com/2008/07/30 /inside-professor-obamas-classroom/.

effect, this particular law professor is asking his students to learn how to teach in order to learn how to learn; he requires students to model for their peers an evenhanded attention to nuance and hard evidence; he listens for the conduct of reasoned debate. Sounds like someone who could do things not just for that tiny state constituted by the pedagogical contract but for a city or state government. Maybe he ought to get into politics.

We can't be there with students when they're drafting an essay or studying for an exam, not most of the time, at least. And we shouldn't be. They need the space and the provocation to struggle through the work. They need for it to be their responsibility. But the classroom offers us an opportunity to witness their struggle, hear their thought processes, and nudge them toward something better, a new or different way to approach something. One of the basic rules of storytelling is that we want to see characters transformed by their experiences, reformed in the crucible of significant events. A classroom is a place where all sorts of stories happen, and the students are the protagonists.

And because learning's goal is for students to be able to do things better than they could before, we need to find ways for class time to be practice time. And for practice to be effective, we need to make audible our students' attempts to get it right. If you've ever been a music student, however briefly, you'll know how important a practice room is. That small, acoustically insulated space, big enough for a piano or bass or trombone, is safe from prying ears so that you can make all the necessary mistakes. Hours are spent there, going over material again and again, as the movements of eyes, hands, mouth, and limbs become second nature, just in time for your intelligence to begin interpreting the music. Technique first, interpretation to follow. A teacher joins you and comments, first on the one, then the other.

The classroom—our classrooms—are practice rooms. In them, we teach techniques of learning so that informed, reasoned ideas—that's the interpretation part—can follow.

So what *does* learning sound like? What's the sonic character of a "good class"? How can we hear our students as they go about transforming themselves? It certainly doesn't sound like you soloing for an hour, unless the learning in question is your own learnedness. And it doesn't usually sound like your students taking long solos themselves, either.

Since music is such a useful way to think about sound, let's go further and think of discussion or participation as a sort of music. "The bass player is the key," Wynton Marsalis suggests. "He needs to keep a steady pulse to provide the bottom and to hold the music together."[3] In most bands, other players appear to be the leaders—trumpeters like Marsalis, pianists, vocalists, saxophonists, guitarists. Bass solos are less frequent, typically, than are those of other instruments, largely because of the danger that the collective structure and movement of the music may break down without that consistent beat. It goes without saying, neither audiences nor band mates want a steady diet of bass solos.

If you're any sort of musician, dear teacher, you're the bassist. It may not be the most glamorous job (actually, it's the least). But in the kind of classroom music we're trying to make, it's an essential one that enables the group to improvise and enables individual performers both to practice playing steady and to test the limits of their instruments.

You will urge the ensemble on or slow them down, provide the chord changes, signal the end of a tune. In this kind of music, you all have parts to play, some composed and some

---

[3] Quoted in Paul Berliner, *Thinking in Jazz: The Infinite Art of Improvisation* (Chicago: University of Chicago Press, 1994), 353.

invented on the spot. Group improvisation in jazz narrows in on what we want our classrooms to sound like:

> Players are perpetually occupied: they must take in the immediate inventions around them while leading their own performances toward emerging musical images, retaining, for the sake of continuity, the features of a quickly receding trail of sound. They constantly interpret one another's ideas, anticipating them on the basis of the music's predetermined harmonic events.[4]

Perhaps from modesty, we teachers don't typically admit just what a complex performance a class period is. We've planned what will happen, but what's really happening is the students, who can't give up their own, autonomous selves. It's essential for us to plan, but planning's never enough.

We listen for the thread of the tune, try to draw out the more sonorous lines that emerge and tune out the less, try to give them space to interpret, anticipate, invent, understand. If we don't hear them, we can't play our part of the performance well, because we'll be teaching the students we imagined them to be rather than the students they are.

So we're faced with a difficult task: *to cultivate the listening—yours and theirs—that will help your students achieve the ambitious work set out in your syllabus.*

We all know that sometimes, through their fault or our own, or through circumstances beyond our control, we just can't hear our students. Like anybody, they often don't say quite what they mean. Like anybody, they sometimes say things primarily because of how these things will make them appear to others. Or they speak out of turn and wear down our ears. Sometimes we're just tired, distracted, or single-minded. Sometimes we're not communicating.

[4] Ibid., 349.

We get a sense of their learning from the work they hand in, but it doesn't reveal all. It doesn't show them trying to learn, in the moment. The evidence of learning is in documents, but it isn't in documents alone. We also have to listen, and listen in ways that can be unfamiliar, even counterintuitive.

Part of why we must listen is that our syllabus had a hand, however large or small, in whatever students are saying. Our design led them here, lit a fire under their interest in Chinese art history, or statistical methods, or Irish drama, and, we hope, called them to speak. Of course, this doesn't always happen for every student. But we're trying to make it happen for every student, and it's already *trying to happen* in every student who's motivated. We have to listen for the sound that that trying makes.

Learning often sounds like "perhaps," like "maybe," like "I'm not sure if . . ." We hear learning when we hear students pointing directly at specific details in course materials rather than gesturing vaguely at the gist of those materials. Learning typically sounds better from week to week, but it's not always in a perfectly linear progression, as we suggested in chapter 5. It sounds like increasingly sophisticated syntax, as students need "not only . . . but also" and "on the one hand . . . on the other hand." Learning sounds curious, genuinely curious, as students ask questions that feel crucial to them, not just for getting through your class but for getting into an understanding of problems that are theirs as much as they are yours.

Learning sounds like your students trying things out, activities at which they are not already experts. To hear those attempts (here is where two writing teachers remind the reader that *essay* derives from French *essayer*, "to try or to attempt"), we'll have to shift our focus from the right answer to the efforts that lead to the right answer.

What sounds like improvisation is actually a product of lots of smaller riffs, theoretical understandings, embodied knowledge, and only very infrequently genius. It is and isn't being invented on the spot. You want students' contributions during class to show that the work you designed for them is *working for them* and helping them work. So you're listening to hear whether they're using what you gave them, how they're using it, and how they're putting the pieces together.

Sometimes a teacher tells a class directly, "Today, I'm going to be listening for the way you practice the skill on which our last assignment focused. Please don't be offended when I jump in to help you adjust how you're using it; this is like refining the technique of a jump shot in basketball or a riff on the guitar. We can always get better, and it's my job to help."

Framing our listening work this way makes clear what the stakes are for us and for them and can help us pluck out the melody from the noise. Once we're clear about what we're listening for, students know what they're trying to perform, even if they can't do it yet. Later, when they're alone at a desk in the library, starting the evening's work, your classroom listening, remembered, will help them realize that what they're doing isn't busywork, that someone will listen to *their* work, too. Their concentration will strive to operate within the range of possibility your listening defined. And, frankly, they may want to try to impress you, assuming you've shown you're capable of being impressed by student work—and that may be unusual for them.

Good classroom listening is reciprocal. Your listening inspires theirs. A highly regarded parenting book is called *How to Talk so Kids Will Listen and Listen so Kids Will Talk*. Teachers aren't parents in the classroom, but the same basic rules for communication remain.

Because one way that students learn is by listening to others—their peers, experts they encounter through course materials, and, yes, you—the teacher can't be the only example of someone doing the thing we want students to do. This communicates the wrong message. We communicate our belief that knowledge is a group project—many-headed, many-voiced—by demonstrating our fascination with and admiration for the way others work and think, and by showing respect for approaches different from our own.

Learning through imitation: These other voices allow students to see many variations of the thing you're practicing together. You put them in your syllabus because you thought they were worth the effort, so to see this effort and make sure it's happening to the fullest of everyone's ability, you find ways for students to practice understanding out loud. You do this so that students will become more comfortable with the way our disciplines make and process questions.

Thirty years ago, the influential Chicana-studies scholar Gloria Anzaldúa taught feminist theory at the University of California, Santa Cruz. The syllabus for her class went on for pages, spelling out readings and commenting on both the conditions and goals of her classroom. Concentrating on third-world feminism, Anzaldúa sought to unlock a system she saw as too white, too middle-class to acknowledge, much less incorporate, the struggles of women of color. Her multipage syllabus arranges readings in a sequence keyed to the topics of class discussion and analysis, but of particular interest are what are functionally headnotes to each part of the document. What makes women of color different from white women, she asks? Speaking as a Chicana and a feminist, she argues that: "We write under crucial states of emergency, internal and external pressure hovering over us to get things out. Consequently the writing is often rough, unpolished, not crafted along traditional lines and that in itself has a power."

Times and circumstances change, but when there's a sense of urgency, there's a sense of power—either power to be resisted or power to be expressed. Anzaldúa's syllabus for this course is filled with commentary and analytic tips that add

III. Literature compensates for a lack resulting from cultural constraints, it is a literature of desire which seeks that which is experienced as loss and absence (as does fantasy—R. Jackson, p. 3)

It focuses on that which is outside dominant value system. It traces the unsaid/unseen of culture, that which has been silenced, made invisible, covered over and made "absent" (Jackson, p. 4)

Use of English, the laws of the dominant culture means accepting its norms. Colored literature is set against the category of the "real" official culture, a category which colored feminist literature interrogates by its difference (Jackson, p. 4). The tension between laws of dominant culture and resistance to that culture and its laws. It has a subversive function. It interrogates the official culture. Its presence is a disturbing confrontation with it and its existential ills. We write under crucial states of emergency, internal and external pressure hovering over us to get things out. Consequently the writing is often rough, unpolished, not crafted along traditional lines and that in itself has a power. Because of economic and social status of our lives, our writings need to get out, hence the urgency. We're all familiar with political revolutions and scientific revolutions but we hear very little about literary revolutions. Lesbian/feminists of color are the conveyors of the literary revolution. The Chicanas are presently having a renaissance. It's the women of our culture who are making themselves and their writings felt.

Excerpt from Gloria Anzaldúa's syllabus. Courtesy of the Nettie Lee Benson Latin American Collection, University of Texas at Austin.

up to a pedagogical philosophy. It's hardly an out-of-the-box syllabus for a women's studies course, as this excerpt shows, because what might be a straightforward catalogue of reading assignments has been tuned for her particular students by a teacher who knows the value of tuning.

Your discipline will have its own sonorities, its own licks and harmonic progressions that sound right. But it will also have its own combinations of notes and instruments that just don't work: There are reasons you seldom see a saxophone in a symphony orchestra.[5] A physical chemistry teacher may lis-

---

[5] Seldom, not never. Berlioz, Debussy, Ravel, and Gershwin are among the saxophone's symphonic patrons.

ten for different things than an architect or a data scientist. A comparative-literature teacher wants to hear something different from what sounds good in a psychology classroom.

Sometimes we hear students saying things that can, if we don't intercede, undermine the careful planning in a syllabus. Sometimes, especially when we're first learning to teach, we either can't fully recognize what we're hearing or don't have the confidence to offer necessary criticism of something we've heard. But left unchecked, a student's sloppy contributions to a discussion can misdirect a whole room of peers. A student's immodest or selfish approach to discussion can, as we suggested in writing about classroom communities, sap the room of that precious commodity, intellectual generosity.

Sometimes a bad sound just happens. If discussion has landed in a particularly rough place, it may be too late for the teacher to do much about it. That can easily happen when the teacher isn't keeping everyone (including him- or herself) honest—*no more bass solos today, please*—and may not have had a plan for where the discussion needed to take the students next in their learning.

Let's repeat that a different way, because we've all made this mistake, and we've probably made it a lot: *Discussion nearly always needs to have a goal in mind*; otherwise it's unlikely to teach students what we want it to. In fact, purposeless discussion frequently gives students the *wrong ideas* about how to do the work of a course, as unfocused opinions drown out the voices of students doing their best to work directly with the intellectual problem of the day.

"No" is a big sound and powerful tool. We use it when what we're hearing tells us we must. We use it so we can finally say—and only when we've earned it—"yes."

So listen well, and make your listening the core of your presence in the classroom. Let's remember that our ears, and not our mouths, are at the center of our heads. Our syllabus is about what students do, so when we're in class, let's try to hear it.

What Teaching Sounds Like

What should we be listening for *from ourselves*? Many of us are uncomfortable hearing recordings of our own voice, a phenomenon that suggests our lack of familiarity with how we sound to others in the everyday. What do *we* sound like when we're doing our work well? What sort of rubric should we follow in determining our own participation grade?

When we were thinking about hearing learning, we went down to the unit of one-on-one learning, the thing that's often called tutoring, a word that doesn't quite capture its spirit. It might be helpful, then, for us to consider how we can hear teaching at that smaller unit, too—our hydrogen atom of pedagogy—which means we should think about office hours, what we do with them and what they can teach us about the sound of our own voice in class.

Office hours are most college teachers' primary experience of one-on-one teaching. We love office hours and we hate them. They signify something special about higher education in the way they give students direct access to us outside of class. This suggests that we college teachers regard our students as young adults, not kids, people with whom we can start to carry on an intellectual relationship that merits this time sitting across a desk from one another. Many of us had a formative experience of the professor who took the time to make us a cup of tea, got to know who we were, and then helped us figure out what our minds could do. For us teachers, office hours are a unique opportunity to learn something about our students, and we often find that a student will communicate differently in class after a particularly good one-on-one conversation. Getting students to office hours early in the term—easily done on the pretext of discussing the syllabus—is for many teachers the open secret for quickly shifting the sound of the classroom.

But this doesn't happen on its own. We go through the first four weeks of class without catching sight of a student in our office—unless maybe someone not even in our class sees the open door and asks a question about degree requirements or where to find a particular office on campus. Then, when it's crunch time, our students show up all at once, demanding more than we can or should give. After crunch time, they might show up again, this time to complain about grades. Sometimes students show up without any real goal in sight, seemingly just hoping to ingratiate themselves with us, or for reasons they don't immediately reveal. This can happen for good and bad reasons, but it can sometimes be difficult to move these encounters from time-sinks to something pedagogically meaningful for the student.[6]

A typical syllabus addresses office hours with a single line, "Office Hours: M 9–10, TH 1–2." But have you explained what office hours are for? If not, students will fill in the gaps with their assumptions about what kind of space your office is going to be for them. We've described the challenges implicit in students' familiarity with the classroom—the way their prior experiences sometimes distort their expectations of what will happen when they come to *your* class. Office hours are a somewhat different problem, as students typically arrive at college without much experience of the teacher's office as a space for learning. Teaching a third-year seminar, one is often shocked

---

[6] Let's not forget that sometimes a student just needs a friendly face and voice. Because we don't know why the student has shown up doesn't necessarily mean the student didn't need that encounter. It's rare that time spent with a student, especially when at the student's request, is time spent without purpose.

(then not shocked) to hear from students who have never visited office hours—for any class—before.

We can, and some of us do, help our students learn how to use office hours by including in the syllabus a more robust address to what they are, what they're for. "All students are strongly encouraged to make use of office hours, early and often. Please arrive with specific work on which you'd like my help, as well as the clearest understanding you can come to for why you're struggling with this work. Office hours are also an opportunity for you to *help me* understand what's happening with all of you students, so please come with a spirit of generosity, expecting generosity in return." Each of us can, if we try, name just what we want office hours to do for students, so why not go ahead and tell them in the syllabus?

We're talking about office hours because we want to hear teaching. Let's imagine that our syllabus has indeed nudged students toward using office hours for learning. Here they are, now, across the desk.

We start with pleasantries, a few questions about how they're doing. This is important work for office hours, important work for teaching, but it can't become the main work.

We ask, "What are you here to work on today?" Teaching sounds like that. We say, "tell me how you got to that idea" or "to that solution" or "to that interpretation." Teaching sounds like that, too. We say, "I noticed that here"—we point somewhere in their work—"you refer to the text from last week, but you don't actually quote it. Where *exactly* are you looking? Can you show me, right now?" The student pulls out the text, finds her way to a page, and reads aloud. You ask more questions, and whenever she gets somewhere, you point at her notebook: "Write that down!" *Like the classroom, your office is a place where students work.*

Like good student participation, good teacher participation is usually specific to the task at hand. For them, it means working.

For you, it's helping them make better work. The more closely and carefully we can point right at something they've done and challenge them to do it better, the more likely it is that our speaking was worth their attention. What we say in office hours, if we stay focused on student learning, is usually a series of questions that respond to what students are doing right at that moment, with us.

It's a series of questions because it leads to more work by them and more questions from us, in a progression, a sort of Socratic or quasi-Socratic method. Our teaching sometimes sounds like each of these methods; we use both. Socratic questioning gets students to carry themselves somewhere *we know* they need to go. Quasi-Socratic questioning gets students to carry themselves somewhere *they'll discover they need* to go, a place we can't entirely anticipate for them.

Like the office, the classroom demands that our participation enable them to find a way to work better, and, as we've suggested throughout this chapter, this is a harder task when there are so many people trying to learn at once. Your questions can't always respond to individual students or point to work that seems right for just one person. Sometimes, nearly always, students are struggling with different things. But it's also true that if you've designed the work of the term well, there will be some things with which most or all of your students are struggling at once. We try to give as many of them as much of what they need as we can. That's what good teaching sounds like.

We can't always ask questions. Sometimes we have to speak for a while to give them something we think they need. Lecturing works best if it still, somehow, resembles a question. One simple way to angle one's role as a teacher is to frame the lecture component of a class in the form of a question. The causes of the Civil War are many and complex. How can we understand the importance of the Civil War, and its causes, in its own time and in ours? Declaratives, interrogatives. It's important, though, that the interrogative challenge isn't a mask for the same set of prepared statements. Opening the lecture part of a class with a big question works better when the answers aren't in the teacher's pocket, best when only some answers are immediately available and others yet to be worked out collectively by the classroom community. With the right lecture-question (let's think for a moment of that as the formula), each class will shape what you have to say in different ways because the classroom community will be composed, semester after semester, in different ways. What's important is that the lecture-question portion of the class always be connected to what follows.

A question causes something to happen *next*. Good lecturing does, too. A lecture is really a form of participation in which the teacher engages, a voice calling other voices, ultimately, to speak. A lecture can be more bass line than bass solo.

Done well, the lecture-question can generate good sounds. If not, not. If we make them wait too long, or they realize we never really imagined they'd say anything meaningful back in the first place, students check out. If our own utterance is the final word, we're hearing poor participation, from them but mostly from us. A lecture can be an extended bass solo, still, too. We strive for something better and more modest not because we have some sort of obligation to hear students' opinions—the world is full of far, far too many opinions—but because we are obligated to listen to students doing something with what we just gave them. Why else would we have given it to them?

Bass solos hide in unexpected places. We might mistakenly assume that because we are responding to a student's question, we are necessarily participating in their learning. We forget that our answer also needs to be a question, needs still to point back toward something the student will do with that answer. Not just call and response, but call and response and response.

Together and Apart

And response and response. What does a community sound like? Let's listen first to the word itself, which, like most words, has a lot to say. From Latin *communitas* down through French to the English word *common*. "Common" meaning neither ordinary nor vulgar and of little use, but "common" as in shared. And shared as in put to different uses—like a village well, from which the same water is drawn by unique, quite separate individuals. What is held in common—a village green, a department's copier—is owned by no one exclusively but by each member of a group, all of whom are very different people with very different uses in mind for the village green/copier. The group sets up rules; the group enforces them.

The dystopian version of the community is groupthink, which happens when the impulse to work together erodes the unique strength of the individuals who make up that group. We know the political consequences of an overwhelming desire for conformity.

The classroom is meant to be nothing like this, at least not in any but the most oppressive regimes. When what we're suggesting here works—and we believe it's a lot easier to make it work than you might at first think—the classroom community understands that a learning group is only as effective as the recognition of the differences among the individuals who make up that group. Standards, requirements, assessments, and other evaluative tools are meant to help each student work and learn *individually* while at the same time working and learning together *within a group*. And that requires listening to two kinds of sounds.

In modern usage, the word *organization* has for so long been fused to business models that there's a pedagogical pleasure in unveiling its origin in the Greek word *organon*, "an instrument for acquiring knowledge"—literally, a tool.[7] Instrument, tool: medical, financial, musical, pedagogical—as teachers, we're in the instrument business, right alongside captains of industry, the operating table, and the conductor's podium.

Our classroom is an organization—an instrument for learning, composed (like music, like writing, like the state of psychological harmony) of different people, whose difference itself makes a learning community possible. A teacher works to make solos happen, student by student, as well as duets, trios, and more ambitious ensembles. There are plenty of times for silence in the classroom, especially when students are being tested, or asked to write, or to read silently and with a purpose. In those lecture-question moments, the teacher wants the only voice filling the room to be her or his own. That silence is the familiar sound of pedagogical discipline at work. But so is the sound of students investigating a claim or a text, pressing the terms of an experiment, exchanging views about a social problem.

By itself, the syllabus does none of this. It's up to the teacher to turn the syllabus into an instrument—a piece of the pedagogical organon—that allows for the buzz of the active classroom, the sound of a group working together. All those voices, and never quite a chorus. That's fine. It can be loud, even raucous, and for the confident, effective teacher, that's music to the ears.

---

[7] *Merriam-Webster Online*, s.v., "organon," accessed July 29, 2019, https://www .merriam-webster.com/dictionary/organon. Aristotle's six works on logic, collectively anointed the *Organon*, are a foundational instrument in philosophy.

8

For Your Eyes Only

Building a syllabus doesn't end when the course
begins. What kinds of writing might you practice
during a semester, after your syllabus is ostensibly
finished, to aid your teaching? What would happen if
you began to think of teaching as a writing process?

In the last chapter we asked that you think about teaching
and the work of the classroom in terms of sound: the art of
teaching—or at least part of it—as the art of listening. This
chapter shifts from the ears to the eyes. Not the scopic re-
gime, that system of controlling by watching (cue your inner
Foucault here, or not), but a way of seeing that's receptive to
what's really going on in your course, a kind of looking that
good teachers do. This isn't exactly a chapter about trade
secrets (which they're clearly not, since you're reading them
in published form)—it's fine for everyone to know that what
we're recommending here exists—but it is, still, about pedagogical confidentialities.

Here we'll focus on your preparation and your capacity to
make the syllabus you've built work as best as it can within
the classroom community you've been engaged to lead. We
can't imagine a student, or anyone else, expressing concern
that you're holding back the fact that you prepare for each class
meeting. To do that well, though, means finding a space for
yourself, a space where you can look hard at what you and

your students have done so far, a space where you can think about, and plan for, your next classroom encounter.

We're expected to think about what we do as teachers, and most of us do exactly that, if not all in the same way. And not just think, but plan. The syllabus, our taskmaster and old friend, our map and fingerpost, helps us to chart a semester-long project about knowledge-making. Which, of course, turns out to be a more challenging, and more rewarding, undertaking than anyone who hasn't taught might imagine it to be.

If you have taught in grade school or high school, or even in some college-level programs, you may have been required to produce lesson plans—fully articulated, miniature syllabi that cover not a semester but a single class meeting. At the college level, lesson plans are valuable teaching tools, though in many disciplines the idea of using one is likely to conjure up uncomfortable associations of junior high and the concerns of local school boards.[1] We want to set aside those associations, at least as much as possible, the better to reinvent the idea of the syllabus as itself a tool for learning (that organon we looked at in the last chapter). Tool, not magic wand. Tools get dented, rusty, lost—at least that's been our experience. Mainly, though, tools are there to do work. Tools that don't do work are either museum artifacts or hipster decor ("I love what your designer did with that adze next to the Victorian love seat"). And a tool performs work because you work with it to make that happen.

A syllabus, though, isn't an adze or an angle grinder or a gimlet. It's a tool that both does work and creates more work. If you began reading this book in the hope that it would make

[1] One of us recalls an otherwise excellent junior high teacher who wrote, in the corner of the blackboard, "Building spelling power." She later confided that she'd done this just in case the principal wandered by and peeked through the classroom door's small window. At one time or another, everyone who teaches feels anxiety about the lesson plan and classroom observation.

your job faster and easier, you'll know by now that we see the syllabus as key to making your job a tiny bit harder but much more effective, and more effective in the only way that's important: as a means of making learning happen.

We're big on understanding and clarity, though we've tried to avoid the term *transparency*, which has become pretty meaningless through overuse. In fact, we're going to suggest, as the title of this chapter indicates, that a successful teacher needn't share absolutely everything with a class. You might imagine the fully transparent teacher putting online working notes for the class or teaching notes on the readings or the notes to self that were discarded in building the syllabus, and you might wonder whether such a portfolio of drafts and rest stops would constitute some sort of fully communal teaching ideal. It wouldn't. Even if such a portfolio were uploaded, it would still have to be taught, and that would mean designing a pedagogy to teach it.

A teacher is entitled to make mistakes and to build on them. That's how a syllabus is worked out on the drawing board and how class preparation notes are derived. As teachers, we need a place to work through our ideas without necessarily sharing every one of them, in all their developmental stages, with our students. They, after all, expect us to be organized, and that means choosing the right tools and materials, not simply throwing everything at them—broken parts, prototypes, laser levels, and ferrules.

So we organize our ideas and our teaching tools in order to make teaching and learning possible. We've said a lot about the syllabus, which may suggest that it's something perfectable. But of course it's not. The syllabus may look set in stone (a wonderful if uninterrogated phrase—what was the last thing in your life that was actually set in stone?), and for your students it may seem to be exactly so. But it isn't—and never can be—at least not for you, at least not for you when you're teaching well. So you plan, sometimes out loud and with your students, but most of the time privately.

Ian Fleming situated agent James Bond in thrilling and picturesque peril again and again. In 1960, a collection of his short fiction included the title story "For Your Eyes Only," cementing in the popular imagination the connections linking top secrecy, glamorous adventure, and danger. This was before social media, against which Bond would face difficulties of a different order of magnitude, but we still have this phrase, this concept of the confidential document, the thing that must not be reproduced, much less shared. In fact, in the era of social media, when platforms and programs call upon us to publish our thoughts in a near constant stream, writing in private is a luxury and an act of resistance. It's also a way to maintain sanity. Adventurous and dangerous though a semester of teaching can be, there is no other agent, no M, dispatching secret missives to guide us in our struggles.

Instead we have the syllabus, which is, of course, nothing like a classified document, or a diary or a journal, for that matter. We give it out, we turn it in, we download it, we get downloaded. And yet the open, available syllabus has an unpublic twin. Whether or not you fully activate them both, the syllabus implicitly exists in two versions: the version for distribution, and the version you keep for yourself. For your students, the syllabus is road map and snapshot. Take a fifteen-week semester and plot out fifteen weekly, or thirty semiweekly, class sessions. The syllabus declares what each class session will be about. It might even indicate what students will do or be expected to have done. "Review of chapter 4. For the next class, be sure to have read chapter 5 and posted your weekly response." There's little downside to repeating those very words in class, just to be sure the message gets through.

What the syllabus almost never says, though, is what the teacher will do or will have done. Every successful teacher is immersed in an academic balancing act—of both scripted and unscripted things to be said, difficult and easy tasks, group and individual projects, and the call and response of instructor and students. One class ends, and that same teacher is also in search of the balance between under-preparing and over-preparing for the next class session. Too little prep is obviously treacherous; too much is, too, even if it feels as if the students will get so much more from the abundance of the teacher's voluble, blackboard-annihilating torrent of information. It's just as possible to *over*-teach as to *under*-teach. It's also possible to not look both ways—backward and forward—when crossing the syllabus, as if it were a highway. You don't risk being hit by a laundry wagon when you're in a classroom, but not looking both ways—at what went well or not in the last session, and what you hope to accomplish in the session ahead—creates structural impediments to successful teaching and to building a productive class.

Think of your critical document, then, as not one single syllabus but two: one for your students, and the second one for you—a copy on which you make notes, changes, ideas, suggestions for another reading, but also the accretions of normal academic life (a student's email address, the room number for a lecture you plan to attend, the title of a relevant new book you need to chase down, etc.). That second, secret syllabus may not be a marked-up, physical copy of your syllabus at all. These days, it's often in digital form, since it's going to grow. You might even bring your laptop to every class, just so you can have easy access to your in-process notes on how the semester is going. This is the secret syllabus as the teacher's other self, a best-informed companion, the personal assistant you never want to be without.

Or, alternatively, your copy of the course syllabus is tucked carefully away in a folder and you *never look at it again*. Which means you take no notes on what you're doing, or what they're doing, on what went wrong or even on what went triumphally right. That leaves entirely up to you the job of re-creating—from memory, a year later, or maybe more—the sequence of questions and exercises that made that triumph possible. It's an open secret of higher education that not every teacher makes teaching notes, that some may be relying instead on a career's worth of accumulated knowledge and experience—decades of introducing students to the fundamentals of social psychology or Early American history—to rekindle the spark needed for every single class.

Some teachers—and among them figures of considerable experience—treat the syllabus as little more than a public disclosure: "Here's the official description, though of course my presence in the classroom is what you've signed up for. Do the reading, come prepared, and we will encounter ideas together, intensely, intensively." At least that seems to be their game plan. If those teachers even have a second copy of the syllabus, the secret is safe with them.

Good teaching strategies? Bad? Surprisingly (maybe), we're sympathetic to the teacher who produces a good syllabus and never looks at it again. Although this approach can sometimes lead to unproductive pedagogy, we recognize in it a reaction against what some teachers perceive as intrusive administrative oversight. One of our goals is, in fact, to persuade those teachers to think of the syllabus as a thing they ought to defend *from* the administrative class, to own it as something critically useful *to the teacher, not the institution.* It's hard to use the syllabus as the teaching tool it's meant to be if you regard it as a capitulation to bureaucracy. Worst case, and you didn't hear this from us (wink, wink), produce one drab syllabus that checks all the administrative boxes to deliver to your department head and another you can really believe in for your real audience, your students. Still, if you want to refine your design for the term, that's not quite enough.

The Instructor's Copy

Back in grade school, there was a textbook for us, the students, and a different textbook for the teacher. We soon learned that that magical tome, the Instructor's Copy (sometimes with a special sticker on the front cover that read INSTRUCTOR'S COPY, just so there was no confusion) contained *the answers*. We couldn't know then how little those answers amounted to for any teacher worth her or his salt—those weren't the answers to the real problems the teacher would face, namely the problem of helping the students in the room *get the right answers*.

There was, however, always another Instructor's Copy, one that didn't announce itself as such. Those were the notes the teacher—a good teacher, at least—kept on what had happened and would happen, how the day would actually be organized and how the day turned out.

And so the most important junior high school lesson for the next generation of teachers may be simply this: Teaching takes preparation, a quality of investment in mental labor, to ensure that the multiple events of any class session can make productive sense. Good teachers, in other words, don't just teach—they think hard about teaching.

Even if the course you're teaching next term comes with an Instructor's Copy, you'll be thinking far beyond the answers it provides.

If you don't already keep a secret syllabus, you can start modestly. Begin by taking notes on how classes are going, week by week—what went well and what didn't. Build on what you already do. In disorganized moments, those notes may be nothing more than a random email you send to your own address or a scribbled note ("This was too tough for them! DROP THIS READING!!!") or even a paragraph you type out for yourself in the fifteen minutes that pop up when a student cancels an appointment.

Keep at it. Give in to the temptation to write yourself longer and longer memos on what happened in this class and what you want to happen in the next. Open yourself up to auto-critique: These are notes by you to you, not a document for your employment dossier or a posting to Twitter.

> "I talked too much again."
>
> "The connection to the work we did last week opened up a conversation I hadn't seen coming. It was exhilarating, but I needed to be in better control of the discussion that took place. Next time: stop the discussion and have them write for five minutes on the author's perspective and what assumptions they can tease out. Then put them into small groups for five minutes. Only then let the conversation turn to the big questions they raised today."
>
> "Review the iPhone images I took of my blackboard notes."
>
> "Add link to the article mentioned in class."

Go ahead: Confess, ponder, and (at least once in a while) congratulate.

> "What a class! The map made all the difference—work up maps for the other three units and post them to the learning module."

This habit of taking notes—the way the doctor takes notes after examining a patient—needn't be excessively time-consuming. A simple twenty-minute jotting after class should fall on the same day that class took place. Now try writing about that moment in some detail, along with an explanation of what made it successful. Does that sound like extra, avoidable work? A year, a semester after the fact, capturing this thinking becomes an impossible task; even a week later, the light has rapidly dimmed.

What is the thing we need more than anything else if we want to be good teachers? *Time to think about what we do as teachers.* Is there a more precious and rarer commodity in academic life? We need the time to write about teaching for the same reasons we take notes in performing our research: If we don't write them down—our mundane observations, plans, and insights—they may float away or never even occur to us in the first place. Take notes on what you've done and what you want to do. As many notes as you can. As often as you can. Reflect, criticize yourself, bask in a moment of self-congratulation when the new thing on your syllabus turns out to have worked. Share that good news with a colleague, if you like. Keep in mind that nothing guarantees that the thing in your syllabus this year will work exactly the same way next year or the year after that. Above all, though, make notes, just as you might advise your students to do when they're trying to craft a paper or carrying out a lab experiment. The great class, like the great paper, comes from a process rather than from some single moment of brilliance. Much of this book has focused on how a syllabus can design opportunities for students to reflect. We'll focus here, though, on your own powers of reflection and a process we'll call *reflective teaching.*

Reflective Teaching

Reflective teaching is just a name for the process of thinking out why you're doing something—your goals for an assignment, what you envision your students doing with it, and what you might then have the group do with whatever the students did in fact do with it—and why something worked or didn't. Reflective teaching isn't about a leather chair by a window that looks out onto the manicured quad. It's about talking to yourself—out loud if necessary, but definitely on paper or in an electronic file—about what worked or didn't and what that success or failure impels you to do next. For most of us, time to reflect isn't an interval that just happens: It's got to be built into what we do. When we ask our students to reflect on a set of readings or an object of analysis like an architectural plan, we want them first to *quote the text*, to be very specific about what they're studying, to make sure they're not misquoting or misrepresenting what's actually there. We want them to point directly at the evidence they're considering and reflect on it in such a way that we can see clearly how they're getting from the thing they're looking at to the thing they're saying about it.

Genuinely reflective teaching records details—the nitty-gritty of a prompt or a problematic interaction that resulted from a complex classroom activity. Reflective teaching isn't grading yourself for your own work in the classroom that day ("I went in expecting I'd be doing B+ teaching but I did solid A teaching!"). It's detailing what specifically concerned the teacher going into the classroom and what activity went well and why. You can give your students a check or check-plus for low-stakes or no-stakes work in class, but you can't do the same with your own classroom work. The point of reflective teaching is to strengthen the acuity of your powers of observation and your analysis of the pedagogical exchange. It's nice that you feel great about a successful class, but it will be a lot more valuable to you—now and in the teaching ahead—if you work to understand what made the successful class successful. It wasn't all your achievement—most of the success may, in fact, be chalked up to what your students did. There were, however, specific things that you did directly or you caused to happen. Take a moment now to think them through.

This can be a difficult task for teachers, who might (optimistically or pessimistically) let what we tell ourselves happened crowd out what really did happen. So we try to get as close to the text as we can—to note what's happening in class, to study the work students hand in. We write one kind of notes *on* student work, and we give those notes straight to the students. We take another kind of notes *about* student work, and we keep these for ourselves, the raw material we'll study in order to figure out what really happened. This is evidence-based teaching in a different sense from what we're used to hearing about in the modern technocratic university. We propose a conception of evidence-based pedagogy that works not from journal articles or "trainings" mandated by HR but from our students' real work. We teach within the peculiar velocity of coursetime, so we can't survey students every week. We can't usually measure their progress mathematically. Teaching's not data science, because reducing to data points everything that our students do will overvalue some things, undervalue others, and leave out far, far too much.[2] This is why we write.

In doing this reflective work over the course of the term, your secret syllabus will grow many times over. You compose a lesson plan—functionally a miniature syllabus—for each class meeting, detailing problems you want to address, things you want to accomplish, and the simple reminders of when work is to be collected and when handed back. Sometimes, typically at the start of the term, you can see the path ahead clearly, and you sketch out a sequence of lessons, exercises, and

---

[2] This isn't to say that quantitative approaches to understanding how students learn can't be valuable. But as we've tried to suggest throughout this book, the insights we gain from such studies can do only so much for real teachers facing the everyday work of designing and teaching a course that will be populated by living, breathing humans.

assignments, plotted down to ten-minute intervals of class time. Other times, especially as you gather more evidence of what's going on with your students' learning, the horizon line is very, very near, and you write out lesson plans an hour before class. This isn't necessarily a sign of poor planning or a sign your syllabus has failed to impose enough order on the term. In fact, it's often a sign your syllabus is working, enabling you to see what students need and to find ways to give it to them.

Many of us are more comfortable when we can build up to a class session, writing our way to a lesson well before the class takes place. Let's say you do this two weeks ahead, a length of time that gives you an opportunity to review the plan more than once. You adjust it as you think about it further, and you're glad you left yourself whatever time you need to make photocopies to distribute or to upload material to the course website. All this is determined by the pacing of their work and yours.

However premeditated your plan, you have it by the start of class. You pull up the annotated syllabus and run through your objectives and problems one last time. Then you teach the class. Immediately after it's over, or as soon as your teaching duties for the day permit, you're back at your syllabus, or that document that began as a syllabus and is increasingly becoming what it needs to be: a teaching diary in which you've recorded the traditional syllabus details as well as your hopes and plans, triumphs and disappointments—*day by day*—in teaching the course. Assuming a fifteen-week term, and no more than two pages of commentary—lesson plan, commentary on what actually happened in class that day—a three-page syllabus can easily expand to more than thirty pages as its bones take on flesh.

That record—we've called it a secret syllabus, but you could call it a teaching diary, if you like—becomes the richest pedagogical resource you can have, an accumulated wealth of mistakes, almost-successes, and near-triumphs. You put your reflections into words, working through the ancient and still mysterious act of taking a living moment and turning it into writing symbols, permanent and meaningful, that you can now return to again and again. From the reflections now attached to your course's syllabus, you've assembled the most important commentary you will encounter on your own teaching. It's even more valuable than an in-class observation by a peer or your chair, which is usually a one-time thing and depends on the predilections of the observer, who necessarily lacks the background knowledge that you and your students have about the course.

When you take these combined notes and reflections, the evidence and analysis of your teaching and your students' learning, and you revise them into a new draft, a draft boiled down to its essence and ready to publish to students, that new draft is the next iteration of your next syllabus, tucked safely away in a digital file, to be awakened at the touch of a finger, ready for the next time you teach the course.

A Teaching Philosophy, with Oranges

By now you know that we think good teaching and good learning are arts that cannot be scientifically determined, pinned to a board, organized within a taxonomy. They're not something you can ever guarantee, even with the best principles. Grand theories of education may be useful, but they'll never quite account for what individual students or particular classes can and can't do.

This means that good teachers are always theorizing for themselves, even if they're also reading about their craft, speaking with colleagues, trying to learn from others and, simply, struggling to be good people—another essential part of teaching. Just as students need to be able to move from the concrete to the abstract in order to build a stock of working concepts, so too do teachers need to move from the real of the classroom to a theoretical understanding of *why* things are happening in the classroom.

In the secret syllabus, we discover—through the act of writing and only because we took the time to write—nonobvious moves we need to make, hidden sources of our failures. We speculate not just about the things that worked and didn't work, for us and for our students, but about the complex sources of our success and failure. *These students are flattening what they read, emptying an argument of its richness, and delivering trite moral lessons in its place.* Why is that happening, and how do we see it happening in action, in the wilds of their (far too domesticated) prose or their comments in class? *These students keep jumping to the wrong conclusions when they analyze sources of experimental error.* The teaching question for us here isn't what they're doing wrong in the finished work—that's usually obvious to us at this point in our careers—it's why they're doing it wrong, how they got to the wrong place.

When we build teaching theories from the raw material of what our actual students are doing and not doing, we inductively reason our way to solutions that make sense in our own, actual classrooms. Every teacher is an education theorist. Some of us are more active in this pursuit, bringing the full weight of our intellectual attention to understanding what our students are doing. Others are more passive, accepting as true the ideas that have been passed down to us—ideas we may not have tested as carefully as we could, ideas we no longer see as the possibilities (not rules) that they are.

But we're not *only* education theorists. We're also expected to be education philosophers, at least in some rudimentary and yet foundational sense. Applications for most teaching positions now ask that you submit a teaching philosophy, a statement that shows your "unique perspective" on how you want your classrooms to run. Our teaching philosophies, though, aren't actually capturable in the two pages allocated in the job application for a "Teaching Philosophy." Our real teaching philosophies are in our lesson plans, our notes, and even, yes, in our syllabus, when our syllabus becomes an outgrowth of the smaller theories we form from week to week, from semester to semester.

By this late stage in the book, you've probably noticed that while we've offered a vision of the syllabus as a place for ambitious teaching and outlined something like our own philosophy, we've left many open spaces for *your philosophy*, the one that will emerge as you reflect on your practice. And we've tried to make the reasons for those gaps clear: It's your class, your students, your subject, your labor, and most important of all, your intellectual and *creative* venture.

Yes, creative. It's no accident that we've compared teaching to composing and performing music, to storytelling, to envisioning a meal (chefs have rightly joined the ranks of artists in the popular imagination), and to the art of politics (even if most politics now falls far below all of these, reduced to crude art indeed). We don't go to restaurants just for nutrition, delivered according to the exacting standards of food science—not least because the nutritionists change their tune every few months.[3] Students don't go to teachers just for form and structure and rules, or they haven't done so in the past.

---

[3] We'll let you finish the analogy to the science of learning. Yes, we now know that eating processed food every day isn't good for us, but anyone who cared deeply about food, especially those engaged in making it themselves, already knew that. Fad diets often spring from science taken out of context, from people looking for an easy answer to complex problems. Most of us don't need experts, or for that matter institutions—from corporations to the FDA—to tell us how to eat.

We worry that in our time, however, students are being encouraged to look for the nutritional facts out of context. Handed a ripe orange, they ask for a packet of Tang, that orange-colored, orange-flavored, sugary powder (100% RDA of vitamin C—why, it must be healthy!).

Many students, especially students carrying with them less privilege, have been handed rotten oranges for far too long—and far too many students still experience that bitter taste even now, in far too many classrooms. So we can't blame them or well-meaning administrators for seeking the surety of factory-tested precision. Tang and other such foods will keep you alive, and a steady diet of mostly artificial ingestibles won't poison you, at least not immediately. But in forgetting what real food tastes like, students risk losing the pleasure of the real thing and—maybe even more important—risk losing risk itself, forgoing the chance to eat something new, at someone else's table, something they made just for us, and the social complexity of that creative encounter. A meal: People coming together, different people, experiencing something we might have mistakenly thought just one of them made, but which they're actually making together.

Repeat the analogy with music, storytelling, and, yes, politics—repeat it with the most human and least human forms of these—and you might hear another tale this book is trying to tell about teaching and its place in our world, now, and about the syllabus and its place in teaching, now.

As John Berger, critic, writer, and teacher, put it, "Art does not imitate nature, it imitates a creation, sometimes to propose an alternative world, sometimes simply to amplify, to confirm, to make social the brief hope offered by nature."[4] Casting the artist as a small (very small) god, Berger suggests that what art hopes for is not to copy a thing already in exis-

[4]John Berger, "The White Bird," *Harper's*, June 2000, 52.

tence. It hopes, rather, to harness lightning and show others that this world is a place of possibilities, that the creation is far from finished. The art of teaching is always about sharing hope, about making it social. The art of teaching is hope, as an art.

You won't tell your students that your teaching is an art, but you hope they will experience it as one. You hope they'll use what you try to give them and use it well, to do good work in the world. You hope, in other words, because as much as teaching is about the urgencies of the present, it's always also about the future.

Here's a teaching philosophy, and it doesn't even take up the two pages on HR's job application form: Teaching is the thing *you* do, with *your students*, and no one else can do it for you. The poet Stephen Dunn once said that our essential experience of life is constant ambiguity: We never entirely know what anything means, what it's for, what it adds up to. So, he said, it's our job as writers to be as specific as possible in order to reveal that ambiguity, to capture its fine details, to open it up and explore it, to look within it for something like the truth. This is why we write about our teaching and how we find some order in the chaos. This is the secret syllabus, and because it's exactly about a semester's work, it's about a lot more, too.

9

—

The Syllabus as a Theory of Teaching

What do you think a syllabus could be, now, after reading most of this book and doing your own writing about the syllabus? What's at stake for students and teachers in the syllabus's form, shape, and status? Who owns a syllabus, really? What do you *want it to be*, and how will you fight for it?

It's not hard to imagine a future—a very near future or even a present—in which our students view their syllabi in the cool blue glow of their laptop screens. They flick their way down the page, scrolling past the endless quasi-legal disclaimers about grading, academic honesty, attendance and lateness, mental health, and on and on, for what would be over a dozen pages—if a syllabus still lived in pages—finally reaching the ubiquitous "I accept" button that they're required to click in order to continue in the course.

The students know little about the contractual obligations to which they've agreed, but they're resigned to the idea that the walls of their everyday habitation must be built out of such legal and technological black boxes. They already click "I accept" every day for all sorts of other consumer goods. The university, having promised that its purpose is "to deliver an excellent student experience" and having successfully lobbied for some industry-friendly changes to the

Family Educational Rights and Privacy Act, is now free to run a little Facebook-like side business mining and sharing student data—or rather to contract that work out to Facebook itself. People don't love this fact, if they even know it, but it helps keep the cost of college down, and everyone else is doing it anyway.

The syllabus we've just described is an "interactive syllabus," where all the course materials and activities are contained within a bright rectangular space that passes for a world. It algorithmically adjusts the activities it requires of individual students, according to their performance and preferences. Or, for a modest tuition reduction, students can agree to let the syllabus adjust activities according to the preferences of a potential employer, suggesting what they "may also like": Netflix for college, college for Netflix. Studies— paid for, of course, by the ed-tech start-up that licensed its course software to the university—have demonstrated a 17 percent increase in student retention and 23 percent better performance on a test the start-up created. Job placement is through the roof. Though the licensing cost was high up front, the new syllabus is so much cheaper to administer in the long term, requiring just one adjunct for every hundred students. It needn't be entirely online: That one adjunct could meet with groups of twenty students once a week, in keeping with "progressive" pedagogical ideas about flipped classrooms and active learning. The assessment is complete: The Orwellian operation was a success, but the patient died.

Such a situation may sound implausible or imminent or something in between, depending on where you teach, what your position is within your institution, and how much time you've spent in recent years reading the *Chronicle of Higher Education*.

A Design for Possibilities

Can a syllabus still be a living thing, even in the strange future that seems to be coming for us? If you teach, you take risks. (If you write, you take risks too, which is one of the things we can teach our students, regardless of our discipline.) Crafting a syllabus involves striking the right balance between things that must be there, things that must happen, and things that *might* be there, that *might* happen. A textbook course is different from a seminar, and each is different from a section of a lecture in which the instructor has some—but not much— freedom to direct what happens in the classroom.

What if freedom and the responsibilities it brings with it were at the front of our minds as we design our courses? We've tried to help you consider that freedom and those responsibilities in the context of the syllabus, a form of writing most of us—the authors of this book included—have at times taken for granted. Our students' idiosyncrasies, and our own, ought to have a home at colleges and universities, in high schools, in any course of real education. If students and teachers and their real work in the classroom are subordinated to some power other than their own collective power to think, we'll have lost the very thing that made us choose to learn and teach in the first place.

We've tried to look at a lot of different ways in which courses are organized and objectives laid out. What every course, and every syllabus, has in common, however, is a balance between obligation and discovery, between required texts and those other readings and projects that you make part of the course's plan. Crafting the right syllabus takes more than subject knowledge: It takes an understanding of what the class must do—and what it *might* do. A good syllabus gives the professor a structure to work with but doesn't become a prison. There has to be a flexible space—for the students, whose response to a course is by definition *not programmable*—and for the professor, who needs to keep options open so that good ideas and enthusiasms can be fostered.

Is a syllabus finally a contract with the student? We've suggested many ways it is—and many ways it isn't. But it's also a launching pad, a springboard into a space none of us can entirely control, at least not in a classroom composed of other living human beings. Mountain climbers, astronauts, archivists, parents, and other explorers know that the unknown is exactly what they've come to find. That's the other part of a course—and of a syllabus: making room for the unknown, taking the risk of driving off the road, at least sometimes.

Which means acknowledging that a syllabus can be a promise but also a wish. What do you wish to happen in your course? The best clues are in the best syllabus. The answers, though, will happen in front of you, in the live moments of teaching, in the community you make.

Us and Them

Throughout the course of this book we've stepped away from the literature on pedagogy, including the daunting archive of work on educational theory. It's not that we think that kind of work doesn't include valuable, if most often technical, insights into the work of the classroom, but rather that we felt it was essential to step back. We wanted to think about our subject in a different internal voice, so that we might produce a different external voice. Education is an urgent subject; writing about education can easily feel technocratic or overly familiar. Learning is a life goal; writing about learning can too easily become bureaucratic and technological and, consequently, a lot less lifelike than it should be.

That said, it's impossible to think, much less write, about the goals and strategies of education without making at least a little space for one perennially modern figure: John Dewey. Dewey's philosophy of education has formed so much of what we do and think that it's easy not to see the presence of his ideas in the educational world that's all around us. In the opening years of the twentieth century, Dewey grappled with the problems not merely of what to teach and how to teach but the bigger questions behind both. We might call those bigger questions the why of the what, the why of the how. This book's grappling with the problem of the syllabus has tried to reach for the why of the what, the why of the how. That's the connection between theory and practice, between goal and strategy and consequence, between the why or how of what we teach and what roles—and there are many—our students play in the complex ecosystem of ideas that we call the classroom.

Dewey had much to say on these questions, and much of what he had published by the time of his death in the early 1950s wades deep into our contemporary debates about the value and values of education. Some of Dewey's most powerful thinking about the why of what we teach is found in a book called *The Child and the Curriculum*. Here he's talking about children, not college-age young adults. The book is well over a century old, yet Dewey's issues are our issues:

> The fundamental factors in the educative process are an immature, undeveloped being; and certain social aims, meanings, values incarnate in the matured experience of the adult. The educative process is the due interaction of these forces. Such a conception of each in relation to the other as facilitates completest and freest interaction is the essence of educational theory.[1]

---

[1] John Dewey, *The Child and the Curriculum* (Chicago: University of Chicago Press, 1902), 3.

But—and this is the crucially important Deweyean *but*—the young student and the value-laden adult curricular subject cannot stand in anything approaching an antagonistic relationship. Which makes sense coming from an educational philosopher who urges us as teachers to see our students as whole, complicated people. The parts of a life are integrated into a person. Real education begins with acknowledging that. Dewey, of course, says it better:

> What, then, is the problem? It is just to get rid of the prejudicial notion that there is some gap in kind (as distinct from degree) between the child's experience and the various forms of subject-matter that make up the course of study. From the side of the child, it is a question of seeing how his experience already contains within itself elements—facts and truths—of just the same sort as those entering into the formulated study; and, what is of more importance, of how it contains within itself the attitudes, the motives, and the interests which have operated in developing and organizing the subject-matter to the plane which it now occupies. From the side of the studies, it is a question of interpreting them as outgrowths of forces operating in the child's life, and of discovering the steps that intervene between the child's present experience and their richer maturity.[2]

Substitute your students, of whatever age, for "child," and the principle still stands. We'll make the substitution here, and requote Dewey: "The [student] and the curriculum are simply two limits which define a single process." That's a staggeringly simple and powerfully generative idea. The process of finding and fostering the life within a student demands recognizing the stuff in that life—what Dewey calls "elements"—and allying them with a curriculum. That alliance cannot

[2] Ibid., 10.

happen, however, if there is no person or persons with whom a student can ally. Learning objectives deracinated from the soil of community make poor allies. Algorithms make still worse allies.

In this book, we've wanted to communicate a sense of the syllabus as more than a skeleton and more than a contract, though it is inevitably both of those things. One of our objectives has been to envision ways in which the teacher can ally rather than align, and use the syllabus as a tool for getting there.

The idea of the curriculum and, for our purposes, the syllabus as an ally and as a plan for alliance runs counter to much contemporary, traditional, well-meaning thinking about teaching and curricular reform. Alignment can be persuasive or coercive—the firmly gentle velvet fist or simply the forceful (always metaphorical, please) fist. As we've tried to lay out in the chapters on feedback and on listening in class, so much of a teacher's job is, inevitably, the task of bringing students to the course's obligations, which means eliciting a conformity to what you want, and in most cases need, to have happen.

Alliance is something else entirely. Allies build together, for a purpose, bound together by an identity frequently shaped in opposition to something else—a position, a force, a system— that stands against or simply stands in the way. So in what sense might a classroom be a place of alliance, rather than alignment? A place of shared purpose, certainly, but to what extent might that sense of alliance be fostered with and through the well-tempered syllabus?

If the classroom can become a place of alliance, the syllabus can be a mechanism for instilling the commonality of purpose necessary for allies to recognize themselves *as* allies, as participants in making students' lives fuller, more complicated, more aware of greater complexity and greater opportunity. That sounds very much like thinking about the classroom at an altitude of thirty-five thousand feet, but there's something to be said for the very big picture. That's where at least one kind of theoretical or philosophical thinking can most easily take place.

Except that real teaching takes place, of course, not at thirty-five thousand feet but at sea level. And sometimes even well below sea level. Teaching is about the murky depths as much as it's about clear skies.

The view from the ground is circumscribed by complex social realities. Your classroom is full of living students; the syllabus is a living document; the work of teaching and learning is in the messy particulars of this life. And the work of building an alliance for learning will appear inefficient if compared—by administrators, politicians, and anyone looking to score easy points—to simpler routes from point A to point B. The destinations at which we arrive with relative ease are the ones Google Maps may suggest—Disney World, Target, Burger King. We access them via an infrastructure that makes such destinations feel inevitable, aided by a GPS that denies us the pleasure of wayfinding, taking the wrong turns that go right. Recall that we used to call freeways, streetlights, and signage *public works*—a term that announced not merely their systemic organization but the collectivity they were meant to serve.

Which is all to say that our path is the students' path, and it's not simply a path to a career or even, for those poor, lucky souls who truly fall in love with learning, graduate school. Our syllabi are designs for possibilities, even when they're also designs for students to acquire definite knowledge or *because* they're designs for students to acquire definite knowledge.

What's the end of a course? Or of an education? There's a desire on the part of many of us to know what we've accomplished each term, through student surveys, through the students' performance on final exams and papers. It seems unlikely, however, that even the best-designed survey instruments can really capture everything that may have taken place over the course of a semester. Some seeds require fire to germinate, waiting years for the blaze that will set them on to new growth; some plants, like the Night-blooming Cereus, bloom only once a year and only overnight. We shouldn't stop trying to anticipate the blooms, to stoke the fires and see what works. But we also shouldn't expect our attempts at measurement to give us a reliable "assessment" of learning. *Measurement, assessment*: These words are nominalizations, verbs that have been (perhaps violently) rendered into nouns. Actions made into things, and relationships made into data.

So, again, what is the end of a course?

The Real Life of a Syllabus

It's much too tempting to work through a book about the syllabus and, upon reaching the final chapter, find that you're thinking about the last class meeting. This book has been a form of thought experiment about the syllabus, but it isn't exactly *a syllabus*. It isn't even exactly a program for remaking your syllabus into something new, whatever *new* might mean at the moment you're reading this. It's been an attempt at understanding what a syllabus is and what it might be, where it helps and where it just gets in the way. That, in turn, opens out onto this book's central and repeated concept: that it's them and not you. It's what they do, not what you do (not so much, at least) that makes a course more than a teacher talking into a mirror.

We realize that if you needed to know how to construct a syllabus for your course, you could have turned to an experienced colleague and asked what worked. *Econ 101?* What's the best textbook? *Intro to comparative religion?* What will the students already know? Where are the third rails? How much theory? *Problems in Baroque art?* I've got favorite problems—what are yours? *Blackness and American urban space?* Is it better to focus on specific cities? What texts teach best? This is how we answer these questions ourselves. There's no substitute for the thoughtful experience of colleagues who have done something like what you'll be doing. Beyond one's home campus, the Web makes possible access to an extraordinary array of syllabi at institutions other than one's own. For anyone building a new course or teaching a subject for the first time, hours devoted to reading up on syllabi for similar courses at schools familiar and unfamiliar is time well spent.

But those are the bones, not the flesh; the trellis, not the vine. Is a syllabus ever fleshy? Vine-y? Or is the lived work of the classroom the thing that grows only in the classroom and disappears when the course ends? If a syllabus is *only* an armature, it's *also* an armature, and on it the work of learning and teaching are made possible in ways that are otherwise very hard. Vines without trellising may wither, shaded out by plants of more upright, but less flexible, habit—or they run wild and choke nearby structures. There are courses of study for which a syllabus may be irrelevant. Learning to swim, for example, is best done in water, not in the library.[3]

What you can't tell from even the best syllabus borrowed from the best teacher is how the work of the classroom moves from bones to flesh. That's the life of the syllabus, and it's about a lot more than classroom learning. We said early in this book that the syllabus, and the classroom that it enables, are about practicing the higher order of adult life. We meant that in particular reference to college and even high school.

Adult-education classes and other forms of post-university study are calibrated a bit differently; their students are already

---

[3] On an episode of *The Big Bang Theory*, resident genius Sheldon announces that, despite never having been in a pool, he has learned to swim by having carefully studied written descriptions of how one holds one's body and moves one's limbs.

deeply immersed in the challenges of adult life, and for them the course of study is about getting to more and different knowledge about the world they've already inhabited for some time. Adult students already know what the younger student does not quite: that the work of learning—anything—is a social project, not merely a factual one.

Or rather, that it's a factual project in the service of a social project, and that the social project is about making a person and making a person-within-society. We call the first the self, the second the citizen. The syllabus can be both the spine and the heart of a course, which in turn makes it a sign of structure and of life. It seems right to end what has been an essay about the life within teaching by emphasizing the ways in which the classroom is preparation for living beyond school. We don't mean job training and professional credentialization, which perform necessary functions in the economy of the modern world, but the work of building on and building from, the continual experiment of learning by being trained in *learning* rather than merely learning facts.

There's always a new semester, always a new opportunity to chart the voyage again, to build the syllabus again, to learn from and with one's students, from and with one's subject. That may finally be the single most powerful, most urgent truth about the classroom and the life for which it prepares.

The Syllabus at the End of the Mind

What, then, has this book been about? What is its premise, if not its own secret syllabus, with its own thought exercises and tentative reorganization of information and ideas into something that readers can make their own? Is it possible, finally, to make statements about teaching—rich, committed statements that can speak to teachers who are scholars and scholars who are teachers, as well as to their students, some of whom are scholars-to-be, eager to become teachers in training? In a book with the no-nonsense title *Syllabus*, we've tried to lay out a controlling idea—it's not what you do, it's what they do—and then to build out from that controlling idea, both backward into how that shapes what the teacher has to make ready, and forward into what happens in the classroom as a result.

We're both trained in literary studies, though in different generations, but with a common grounding in the work that has, over the past twenty years, consolidated itself as the history of theory. Whatever theory was, from the emergence of poststructural inquiry in the late 1960s through its development and complicated dissolution since the turn of the millennium, few of us in the humanities and social sciences speak and think about theory in the way we might have were we addressing theory's nature some thirty years ago. In a moment just before the sunrise of the digital age, the British critic Terence Hawkes made a pitch for theory as a form of knowledge-making that democratized the humanities, since the scholarly resources required by theoretical work were pretty much available in the average college collection. One didn't need the archives of an R1 university to do theory, so the argument went, though theory could be done in those places, too. The rise of the internet has only extended further our access to materials—including precious items from R1 archives—as well as the direct publication online of journals and books, not to mention blogs and other forms of almost-instant commentary. All of this makes many forms of research much, much easier and possibly aligns contemporary ways of knowledge-making with the ideals that motivated Hawkes's embrace of theory.

But what, after all, is theory—any theory—*for*? The work of scholarship, of teaching and learning, concerns itself with the particular and the general, or rather the other way around: the general principle as a means of explaining the particular, even if the general is derived from examining sets of particulars. In its heyday, what was labeled "theory" reached outside disciplinary borders—a set of defensive walls that today seems charmingly quaint—in order to get to some bigger truths about forms of knowledge. In a sense, theory was anti-disciplinary, at least to the extent that its organizing principle was that something about life had to be made clearer. Theory was a new toolbox or a set of experiments for repurposing old tools. It didn't matter if the resistant padlock was in the history of science or anthropology or gender studies. The new tool—new or made new—would open the lock, and in doing so would demonstrate that unfamiliar tools could be of use no matter what you were researching.

We're in a different moment now. Something once labeled "the resistance to theory" now seems as quaint as the high-water mark of dense European philosophizing that once reigned in (and for some academics terrorized) American literature departments. Not a day goes by—not an hour even—without a report in the academy's trade papers bringing more news of the crisis in the humanities or education funding or the student as consumer or the university as an unsustainable enterprise. Actually, it's not news, because it's much the same report over and over, a drumbeat to accompany a march we'd all rather not be on. We know that no degree of theorizing about our disciplines or about the relationship of the state to the Enlightenment's vision of an educated citizenry or about systems of injustice or about the nature of narrative is *in itself* going to ameliorate present conditions. It's not as if the high priests of theory thought otherwise. The point, as a certain German materialist philosopher put it, isn't to account for the world, as philosophers—or maybe theorists—do, but to change it. Not to account for our subjects, or for our students, but to change them—subjects, students—in the best way we know how to: by teaching. If a miraculous teaching moment ever occurs, it is surely when, as David Gooblar puts it in *The Missing Course*, one realizes that *"the students are the material"* (italics his): "If I was going to be a good teacher, I was going to need to master the mysterious art of helping people change."[4]

Researchers and teachers do different things, because scholarship and teaching are different things. But they're not *irreconcilably* different things. Teachers who know they're teachers also know why they're in the classroom. Scholars who also teach, or teachers who devote much of their energies to scholarly pursuits, have a more complicated relationship to the classroom. For some, that relationship speaks to a divided loyalty, while for others it's exactly the tension between making scholarship and teaching that generates the spark. On the best days, the same spark ignites the teacher's work in the classroom and the scholar's work at a laptop, deep in some archive or in the lab.

If, as we've known for some time now, theory will not repair the rent garment of knowledge, what then is to be done? Our answer is: Teach, and teach well. Do better than that. Teach better. Better so that learning—what students get out of it— outpaces teaching, which is certainly what we get out of it, whether or not we're willing to admit that teaching is a source of professional satisfaction precisely because the spotlight and the students' attention confirms the authenticity of the profession we have chosen. Too much teaching may be about the teacher. Teaching too much is definitely about the teacher.

We've been playing here with Hawkes's instinct about theorizing—that it made complex thinking available at low

---

[4]David Gooblar, *The Missing Course* (Cambridge, MA: Harvard University Press, 2019), 4.

cost—in order to make a big move: *Pedagogy is the new theory*. For two generations of academics nurtured on complex theoretical programs in the humanities and social sciences, as well as scholars and researchers in the scientific and technological fields, the very concept of theory is foundational. Pedagogy is that other thing that organizes what one does with students. Yet it takes only a gentle push for the foundational concept to blur into the organizing concept, and for pedagogy's foundational function to wander across an imaginary line to confound theory's explanatory power.

This is our last chance to make absolutely clear that the authors of this book aspire to the thing they're describing here. *Syllabus* is a call to engaged teaching, not an account of the authors' personal triumphs. Far from it. We'll each keep trying to move our classrooms and ourselves in the right direction, and we can't ask more than that of you as you struggle— just the way we do—with teaching's embedded questions of authority, knowledge, generosity, and power.

Power: Both theory and pedagogy are about it, though neither in a simplistic political way. As experienced teachers know, teaching tools—examples, anecdotes, textbooks, concepts, signifying terms, reading lists, syllabi—have their own unique half-lives, and when they stop being sufficiently radiant, that example (anecdote, textbook, concept, signifying term, reading list, syllabus) is set aside and replaced.

The strengths of the theoretical moment are part of the academy's historical record, but one of the most important consequences of that intellectual ferment is surely the way in which thinking theoretically allowed diverse disciplines to introduce larger, more philosophical programs into their field of vision.

In theory's Golden Age, there were probably few academics working on abstract systems to account for teaching itself. In practical terms, teaching has long been the means by which rather than the object of: We've taught in order to inspire students in African history or stochastic modeling or minimalist music. The teaching *itself* has too often been taken for granted.

Over the past twenty-five years, much about the academy—and much about teaching—has changed. There are still scholars in "the disciplines" (we're tempted to add an ironic ™ here) for whom ed schools, and with them the whole enterprise of teaching as an ed-school undertaking, are a separate, and lesser, order of professional work within the university. We want to place the conflict in a different light: What the Golden Age of theory took as its project—to explain events, phenomena, and histories through the discovery of relations that constituted unacknowledged systems—has morphed into the goal of teaching. Or to put it the same way only differently, theory was tough, but it wanted to teach us things, and it did. It wasn't all done well, but theory fundamentally changed us by enhancing our capacity to think abstractly, philosophically, skeptically, politically, and humanely, in the widest possible sense of that last word. The world is still the same damaged place it was before the theoretical turn—in some ways even more damaged, though we have more tools to think with, and to teach with, too.

Pedagogy—the study and practice of teaching—isn't the damage-repairing, budget-restoring, attention-commanding, devotion-inspiring universal tool we want for ourselves and for our students. But the one thing we can do is teach well. And we can make thinking about teaching—which means really thinking about learning, and not merely about our knowing more about our subject—our first and unwaveringly most important goal.

We think we can do it. We think you can, too.

Further Reading

In pursuing this project, we discovered a different way to imagine books about teaching. We read them not as people looking for a straightforward solution to our problems—a single book we could read that would magically transform us into better teachers—but as craftspeople who know there will never be an end to new ideas, experiments, and insights about the delicate social art we practice.

It's in that spirit that we're sharing this necessarily incomplete list of works that we've found helpful, and which you might, as well. Part of what makes this list incomplete is that we've both learned a great deal from books that are *not* explicitly about teaching, from cookbooks to short story collections, from works of history to gardening guides. Sometimes we're able to understand a teaching problem because we read a new analysis of people's relationship to digital devices or a fresh take on color theory.

One takeaway: Books explicitly about teaching are fine, but books that can teach—really teach—show up in unexpected places. Keep your eyes open. We urge you to flesh out this short list with whatever helps you learn how to see your students' needs in sharper contrast.

Ambrose, Susan A., et al. *How Learning Works: Seven Research-Based Principles for Smart Teaching.* San Francisco: Jossey-Bass, 2010.

Bain, Ken. *What the Best College Teachers Do.* Cambridge, MA: Harvard University Press, 2011.

Bean, John C. *Engaging Ideas: The Professor's Guide to Integrating Writing, Critical Thinking, and Active Learning in the Classroom.* 2nd ed. San Francisco: Jossey-Bass, 2011.

Berliner, Paul. *Thinking in Jazz: The Infinite Art of Improvisation.* Chicago: University of Chicago Press, 1994.

Brandt, Deborah. *The Rise of Writing: Redefining Mass Literacy.* Cambridge: Cambridge University Press, 2014.

Brown, Peter C., et al. *Make It Stick: The Science of Successful Learning.* Cambridge, MA: Harvard University Press, 2014.

Davidson, Cathy N. *The New Education: How to Revolutionize the University to Prepare Students for a World in Flux.* New York: Basic, 2017.

———. *Now You See It: How the Brain Science of Attention Will Transform the Way We Live, Work, and Learn.* New York: Viking, 2011.

Dewey, John. *Experience and Education.* New York: Free Press, 1997.

———. *The School and Society and The Child and the Curriculum.* Chicago: University of Chicago Press, 1991.

Evans, Nancy J., et al. *Student Development in College: Theory, Research, and Practice.* 2nd ed. San Francisco: Jossey-Bass, 2010.

Gooblar, David. *The Missing Course: Everything They Never Taught You about College Teaching.* Cambridge, MA: Harvard University Press, 2019.

Halonen, Jane S., and Dana S. Dunn, "Does 'High-Impact' Teaching Cause High-Impact Fatigue?" *Chronicle of Higher Education,* November 27, 2018.

hooks, bell. *Teaching Community: A Pedagogy of Hope.* New York: Routledge, 2003.

———. *Teaching to Transgress: Education as the Practice of Freedom.* New York: Routledge, 1994.

Lang, James. *On Course: A Week-by-Week Guide to Your First Semester of College Teaching.* Cambridge, MA: Harvard University Press, 2009.

Lang, James. *Small Teaching: Everyday Lessons from the Science of Learning.* San Francisco: Jossey-Bass, 2016.

Lindsay, Peter. *The Craft of University Teaching.* Toronto: University of Toronto Press, 2018.

Mazur, Eric. *Peer Instruction: A User's Manual.* Upper Saddle River, NJ: Prentice-Hall, 1997.

Neuhaus, Jessamyn. *Geeky Pedagogy: A Guide for Intellectuals, Introverts, and Nerds Who Want to Be Effective Teachers.* Morgantown: West Virginia University Press, 2019.

North, Stephen M. "The Idea of a Writing Center." *College English* 46, no. 5 (September 1984).

O'Brien, Judith Grunert, Barbara J. Mills, and Margaret W. Cohen. *The Course Syllabus: A Learning-Centered Approach.* San Francisco: John Wiley, 2008.

Warner, John. *Why They Can't Write: Killing the Five-Paragraph Essay and Other Necessities.* Baltimore: Johns Hopkins University Press, 2018.

Index

taste, 106
teacher, the: as an ally, 187; assumptions and, 122; attendance and, 136–38; authenticity of, 45–46, 194; burnout and, 132; copy of the syllabus, 166–70, 173–75; focused class, 3–5; leading students, 52, 90, 132; learning from students, xx, 4–5, 12, 15, 194; motivation of, 40, 44; notes, 167–71, 173–75, 177; in office hours, 155–57; participation, 157–58; preventing cheating and, 134–36; relationship between student and, xviii–xix, 13, 185–86; role in discussion, 148; role in the classroom community, 43, 58; work beyond the classroom, 15, 59, 115–16, 139
teaching: art of, 179; assignments and, 57, 59–61, 93, 110, 116; collaborative, xvi, xxi; failure and, 96, 98, 109–10, 165, 172, 176; genuine theatrics of, 47; goals of, 21, 29, 33, 59, 90, 105, 121, 196; grading and, 116–17, 120–24; how to read, 76, 90; how to think, 91, 101, 103; is hard, 1–2, 17; learning-centered models of, 11–12, 21, 189; lesson planning and, 149, 164, 174, 177; listening and, 149–51, 154, 159–60; online, 136; philosophy, 176–77, 179; politics of, 33; preparation and, 163, 167, 169; to prepare students for beyond classroom, 23, 92; process and, xxiii, 101, 171; providing feedback and, 57–60, 119, 124–28, 131–33; purpose of, 21, 145, 185, 193–94; questions and, 90, 176, 195; reading lists and, 73, 75–76, 83–86, 90, 93; reflective teaching and, 171–76; relationship between student and, xviii–xix, 13; scholarship and, 194; silence and, 34; sound of, 155, 157–58; students how to read, 76; syllabus and, 16, 94, 133, 161, 177; techniques of learning, 148; theory of, 44, 175–76; thinking about, xxii, 17, 98, 176; time and, 49–50, 53–54, 59–61, 65–66, 121, 132–33, 172; tools,

76, 86, 90, 121, 195; top-down, 142; writing about, 11–12, 173, 179
technology, 18, 181
tenure, 120
textbook, 69, 72–73, 111–12, 169, 183
theory, 42–44, 175–76, 184–85, 192–93, 195–96
These Truths (Lepore), 17–18
time, 49–53, 61, 64–65, 172. *See also* coursetime
"To a Mouse" (poem), 112
To Engineer Is Human: The Role of Failure in Successful Design (Petroski), 70
transparency, 164
Trilling, Lionel, 45
trust, 29
tuition, 182
tutor, 145

United States, 17–18, 24
university, the: accommodation and, 31–33; cost of, 81–82, 120, 182; distrust of knowledge from, 18; elite universities and, 120; as a gateway into adulthood, 20–21; hierarchy of, 24, 91; purpose of, 2; requirements of, 64; writing center at, 145. *See also* education; higher education
University of California, Santa Cruz, 152
University of Chicago, 76, 146
University of Michigan, 76
U.S. Constitution, 18–19
use value, 92

Weber, Max, 20
World War I, 6
writing: about education, 184; about learning, 184; about teaching, xvii–xviii, 11–12, 173, 179; assignments, 101; center, 145; in private, 166; a research paper, 111; students and, 16, 58–59, 101; the syllabus, 10, 16, 40, 176; theoretical, 43. *See also* reading
Writing Across the Curriculum, 16